MYTH, MEANING, AND PERFORMANCE

THE YALE CULTURAL SOCIOLOGY SERIES

Jeffrey Alexander and Ron Eyerman, Series Editors

PUBLISHED

Triumph and Trauma
by Bernhard Giesen (2004)

Myth, Meaning, and Performance: Toward a New Cultural Sociology of the Arts
edited by Ron Eyerman and Lisa McCormick (2006)

FORTHCOMING

The Easternization of the West
by Colin Campbell

American Society: Toward a Theory of Societal Community
by Talcott Parsons, edited and introduced by
Giuseppe Sciortino

Contemporary Societies: Self, Meaning, and Social Structure
by Jeffrey Alexander and Kenneth Thompson

Setting the Stage for a "New" South Africa: A Cultural Approach to the Truth and Reconciliation Commission
by Tanya Goodman

MYTH, MEANING, AND PERFORMANCE

Toward a New Cultural Sociology of the Arts

Edited by
Ron Eyerman and Lisa McCormick

Paradigm Publishers
Boulder • London

Copyright © 2006 Paradigm Publishers

Published in the United States by Paradigm Publishers, 3360 Mitchell Lane Suite E, Boulder, CO 80301 USA.

Paradigm Publishers is the trade name of Birkenkamp & Company, LLC, Dean Birkenkamp, President and Publisher.

Library of Congress Cataloging-in-Publication Data

Myth, meaning, and performance : toward a new cultural sociology of the arts / edited by Ron Eyerman and Lisa McCormick.
    p. cm.
  Includes bibliographical references and index.
  ISBN-13: 978–1–59451–214–8 (hardcover : alk. paper)
  ISBN-10: 1–59451–214–0 (hardcover : alk. paper)
  1. Arts and society.   I. Eyerman, Ron.   II. McCormick, Lisa, 1975–
NX650.S6M98 2006
306.4'7—dc22

                                                                                2006000236

Printed and bound in the United States of America on acid-free paper that meets the standards of the American National Standard for Permanence of Paper for Printed Library Materials.

Designed and Typeset by Straight Creek Bookmakers.

10   09   08   07   06
1   2   3   4   5

Contents

Introduction   1
Ron Eyerman and Lisa McCormick

1   Toward a Meaningful Sociology of the Arts   13
    Ron Eyerman

2   Chewing on Clement Greenberg: Abstraction and the
    Two Faces of Modernism   35
    Robert W Witkin

3   The Meaning of Style: Postmodernism, Demystification, and
    Dissonance in Post-Tiananmen Chinese Avant-Garde Art   51
    Julia Chi Zhang

4   Seeker of the Sacred: A Late Durkheimian Theory of the Artist   81
    Steve Sherwood

5   Music as Agency in Beethoven's Vienna   103
    Tia DeNora

6   Music as Social Performance   121
    Lisa McCormick

Bibliography   *145*
Index   *155*
About the Contributors   *165*

Introduction

Ron Eyerman and Lisa McCormick

PRODUCTION, POLITICS, AND MEANING: PREVIOUS PERSPECTIVES IN THE SOCIOLOGY OF THE ARTS

For the past several decades, the sociology of the arts has been dominated by the production of culture perspective, especially in the United States. This perspective takes the social organization of the arts as its prime concern and leaves any question of meaning to the humanities, to philosophers and art historians (see Peterson and Anand [2004] for the latest summation). From such a perspective meaning is either bracketed out entirely, as lying outside the competence of the sociologist, or considered as a function or outcome of that social organization which is the sociologist's proper concern. While this perspective has been particularly dominant in American scholarship, Bourdieu can be said to offer a European variant, where the masters of the grand sociological narrative, Marx, Weber, and Durkheim, are brought to bear on the production of value and the consumption of artifacts as forms of social distinction. Combined with a feminist appropriation of Foucault, which reads artifacts through discourses of power and domination, these sociological approaches to art have spread into art history and other disciplines traditionally grounded in humanism. Here, areas of study such as art history that once sought to uncover the universalistic values that defined great works of art are now engaged in

1

disclosing how such value gets assigned to cultural artifacts—a notion now expanded to include film, video, and television—as the outcome of interactions on discursive fields constituted through power.

While both the art worlds and production of culture of the sociologist and the new art history have in common the contextualization of artifacts, there are significant differences. The prime focus of art historical analysis remains the content of an artwork or a musical composition and the meaning it may convey to an audience, be they local and contemporary or distanced by time and space. Much of contemporary sociology of the arts, on the other hand, brackets out meaning to focus on the context of production, and any "meaning" that may result is taken as an epiphenomenal outcome of the process of production itself, not something internal to an artwork or to any communication between the work and its audience. Thus, while art history can be said to have experienced a sociological turn, incorporating the sociology of art worlds into its analysis of the content and meaning of artworks, sociology has not reciprocated. The sociology of the arts has, until very recently, left such analysis of the art object aside. There are now signs of opening, however, of the emergence of a new sociology of the arts, which would achieve two things: expand the sociological approach to art to include the content, performance, and meaning of artworks, while at the same time expanding its focus to include artifacts from popular culture.

Building on the established research into art worlds, what is interesting for the new sociology of the arts is the relationship between the production of artworks, objects designated as art, and the production of meaning. What meanings and motivations are involved in the production of art objects and communicated in their reception, and how are these related to wider social processes and structures? To take some well-established positions on such questions, for the Frankfurt School, the production of meaning is bound up with the production of cultural artifacts, especially in modern society with its culture industry. From this perspective, the concept of ideology is central to any analysis of contemporary art. The situation is more complex in older, traditional societies and in relation to artifacts identified as being outside the culture industry (i.e., high art). Here the relation between art and social structure, art and values, is considered complex and ambiguous. For example, for critical theorists such as Theodor Adorno and Herbert Marcuse, a piece of classical music can be said to contain a transcendent or critical moment, even when it is performed and heard in a modern context. While early critical theorists were keen to restrict this transcendent or emancipatory potential to high or serious art, younger critical theorists are more open to the possibility that some artifacts of popular culture might also contain something of the same. For the classical Frankfurt School, however, meaning is given in the medium and popular culture is manufactured meaning.

At the other extreme is located the widely divergent field of study known as cultural studies (CS). Cultural studies has largely ignored the Frankfurt School, taking inspiration instead from post structuralism and semiotics. At the same time, CS has reversed the Frankfurt School's position regarding the critical potential of popular culture (Gitlin 1997). For many CS enthusiasts, popular culture is not a source of indoctrination or false consciousness, as it was for the Frankfurt School, but rather a source of resistance to the dominant culture. Some would even go so far as to say that popular culture is *popular* because it is resistant to cultural hegemony (for the reflections of a reconstructed CS, see Morley 1997). Support for such claims were bolstered by ethnographic studies of youth cultures, largely carried out in the UK (see Hall and Jefferson 1976 for the classic statement).

At the same time as it has reversed the valuations of the Frankfurt School, CS has challenged the distinction between high and mass culture that defined the early work of the Frankfurt School. Here, CS clearly finds support in recent developments in the (fine) arts and in mass communications, where the lines that helped define the distinction between high and popular culture are continuously challenged, if not entirely eliminated. With influences stemming from the linguistic turn in theorizing and methods of analysis borrowed from the humanities, CS theorists have looked for multiple levels of meaning and interpretation in cultural artifacts and their reception/interpretation. They have concentrated attention on what are conceived as the decentered effects of mass cultural products such as TV and film, and the aesthetic elements in such blatantly commercial enterprises as advertising. In challenging the distinction between popular and high culture, however, cultural studies has tended to study the former and to neglect the latter, in part because the distinction itself is declared hopelessly out-of-date. Even if one recognizes the difficulty of specifying the aesthetic qualities that separate classical and popular music, however, or a piece of advertising from a Picasso, there is clearly a difference in intention and interpretation between a urinal placed in a museum exhibition hall and the one in its men's room. CS has spent most of its energy in the latter.

Art history has experienced a virtual revolution with the introduction of feminist theory and poststructural discourse analysis (poststructural in the sense that "structure" is modeled on the relative openness of language rather than the closeness of institutions), especially as practiced by Lacan and Foucault (Harrington 2004). As methodology, discourse analysis aims at disclosure through description, not verification or explanation as traditional science. It seeks to uncover the meanings encoded or embedded in cultural artifacts, now conceptualized as texts or as visual culture, rather than high art or literature. The concept of truth is thus bracketed out in favor of multileveled and layered "thick" descriptions. Its concept of power derives from Foucault rather than Marx, implying that power is entwined in assignation, with the right to name, define, see and be seen, and, most of all, speak. In seeking to uncover the meaning encoded in the cultural artifacts, conceptualized as "texts," cultural studies turns to Lacan for concepts such as desire, fantasy, the gaze and the look, for analyzing everything from rock lyrics and soap operas to impressionist painting. The sociology of art has lagged far beyond, with both positive and negative consequences.

On the positive side, proponents of the production of culture approach in the United States have maintained a healthy interest in the social organization of art worlds. Authors as diverse as Howard Becker (1982), Diana Crane (1987), and Tia De Nora (1995) have studied how music and art (i.e., high culture) should be conceived not simply as resulting from the imagination of individual genius but as organized social activity, where individual artists are linked into networks that both limit and sustain their creative acts (see Becker and Pessin, forthcoming, on the differences between the art world and the field of cultural production). In many ways correcting the brilliant analysis of the social constraints on Mozart's genius by Norbert Elias (1993), De Nora demystifies the notion of genius by reconceptualizing it as reputation, something that can be studied as a social process of production. From this constructivist perspective, the organizational structure of an art world is essential to any understanding of a particular art object. Richard Peterson (1997) has made similar observations on a more macro level regarding one of the most popular aspects of American popular culture, country music. Peterson reveals how "authenticity," a core concept in the understanding of country music, was fabricated, produced, and manufactured, as commercial interests searched for stars and themes to which their audience would respond.

What this focus on the social organization of cultural production has been reluctant to consider, and what is the strength of the new art history, is the content and meaning of an artifact, be it of high or popular culture. With its focus on the production and interpretation of text and image through the concept of visual culture, the new art history has expanded its field of vision to include not only film and photography but also a wider range of interpretation than that which focused on the formal qualities of a cultural artifact. "It also means," as some supporters put it,

> that it is possible to approach canonical works, those said to be invested with inherent aesthetic value, with different eyes. Instead of seeking to promote and sustain the value of "great" art by limiting discussion to the circumstances of the work's production and to speculation about the extraordinary impulses that may have characterized the intentions of the makers, [the new approach] examine[s] the work performed by the image in the life of culture. (Bryson et al. 1994:xvi)

While art history and other humanities such as comparative literature have opened to new twists and turns in feminist and poststructuralist theorizing, as well as to a more "anthropological" approach to cultural artifacts, the sociology of art has felt more comfortable to analyze such artifacts from the "outside." This of course is also true of the most influential European in the field, Pierre Bourdieu, as well as the Americans mentioned earlier. In *Art and Social Structure* (1995) and "Constructing a Sociology for an Icon of Aesthetic Modernity: *Olympia* Revisited" (1997), Robert Witkin attempted to move the sociology of art in a new direction in complementing the externalist "art world" approach with a sociology of the "artwork." In so doing, he entered territory previously occupied by art historians (though there are sociological precedents; see, e.g., the newly translated *Rembrandt* by Georg Simmel [2005]), where the content and meaning of the cultural artifact is a prime concern. A "sociology" of the artwork would attempt to relate this content to wider sociological concerns with social structure and social change. Thus, in the article just referred to, Witkin offered an interpretation of Manet's *Olympia* from 1865 that bases itself in the classical sociological concern of the shift from value to instrumental rationality associated with the transition from traditional to modern society. He analyzed that painting in light of the general sociological narrative about the effects of the transition from traditional to modern society and what this meant for social relations.

The thrust of Witkin's argument was to read transformations in social structure and relations as they are reflected in artworks. This was exemplified through a detailed analysis of Manet's *Olympia*. Following art historians such as T. J. Clark and Linda Nochlin, Witkin "read" *Olympia* in its historical and social context, as a critical insider's commentary on the bourgeois male world of late nineteenth-century Paris. What he added to these by now standard Marxist and feminist accounts is the viewpoint of classical social theory, outlined earlier. From the historical narrative provided by classical theory, Witkin located Manet's work in the transition between traditional and modern society and claims that one can uncover not only a more or less conscious attempt by the artist to shock his contemporaries with his choice of subject matter and manner of representation, but also the emergence of a more "abstract," subject-oriented style that would characterize modernism and modern social relations. Such a reading is possible only on the basis of a grand historical narrative, one that, in the spirit of classical social theory, places contemporary events within a broader context of social development.

Witkin has been unapologetic in his return to grand theory in this postmodern era when it has gone out of fashion. His is a post-postmodernism, however, in the sense that Witkin takes seriously some of postmodernism's (including the art historians mentioned previously) objections to grand theorizing of the type he seeks to re-instate. One of these is the call to contextualize, to interpret artworks, among many other things, of course, within their concrete historical settings. Another is the focus on symbols and the value of semiotic analysis. The first calls attention to local knowledge and experience, to the concrete, as opposed to the abstracted discourse of grand theory, as well as to the organizations, decision-making, and power structures that concretely affect the "production of culture." The second refers to the various levels of meaning and interpretation that an art object can contain or involve. The inclusion of various perspectives and levels opens the possibility of several "meanings" and interpretations in a single artwork. Thus, *Olympia* can be interpreted in its contemporary context and in a wider theory of social development. One does not exclude the other, although the latter is more general and more abstract and can thus include the former, while the reverse is not the case. Whether or not this means Witkin's is a "truer" or "better" interpretation, rather than merely a broader and more inclusive one, can of course be discussed. As sociologists, however, our own feeling is that while it may not be truer, it is certainly better.

At the same time as relating art works to social structure, and to classical social theory, Witkin sought to demonstrate that artists such as Manet, working within inherited traditions yet innovating through them, can convey to audiences viewing their works a reflective understanding of themselves and the social relations of their age, where art styles are seen as agents of social change and not merely as reflections of it. Here reference was made to what could be called the "truth-bearing" capacity of art. As part of the meaning they may convey, artworks can evoke a reflexive or cognitive response from viewing publics, in which powerful emotion and re-cognition can combine to produce extraordinary affect. While Witkin (and Bourdieu similarly) focused attention on the responses of individuals, even where these individuals are thought to be class related, it is possible to expand the analysis to include collective action and actors, something pointed to in others' work on music and social movements (Eyerman and Jamison 1998). The door is now opened to new directions in the sociology of the arts.

BEYOND PRODUCTION: UNBRACKETING MEANING, REDISCOVERING MYTH, AND EXPLORING PERFORMANCE

The essays in this volume address many sociological and aesthetic issues. For the purposes of this introduction, we highlight three themes that signal, for us, a new direction in the sociology of the arts: meaning, myth, and performance. While every essay in this volume is centered on the question of meaning, Eyerman's contribution tackles this issue directly by articulating the conceptual steps that would lead toward a new "meaningful" paradigm in the sociology of the arts. First, he demonstrates the need for a new spatial metaphor for art. The problem with more established spatial metaphors of the "art world" and the "field of cultural production" is that they reify the institutional space surrounding art and overestimate external determinants of action and belief. Instead, he suggests that we broaden the sociological view by understanding art as a conceptual or experiential space for imagination, creativity, and critical reflection. In other words, we should understand art as "space within a space, a place to view the surrounding world from, yet not untouched by it." In addition to a different conception of art, a meaningful new paradigm in the sociology of the arts would also adopt a different conception of culture. The purely instrumental view of culture reduces the role of art to distinction and profit and remains blind to the experiential or sociological truths embedded in aesthetic forms. For this reason, he advocates the notion of culture as shared meaning structure that frames interpretation and action without determining them. Culture, like art, should be understood as relatively autonomous, always intertwined but never completely determined by social structure. Eyerman argues that these conceptual shifts would enable a sociological analysis of art that remains sensitive to the meaning of an artwork and the intentions of the artist while still providing rigorous analysis of historical and social context.

The second chapter explores the meaning of an artistic "movement," specifically, the transition from abstract expressionism to pop art. According to Witkin, Western modernist art has been defined by a tension between two equally strong yet antithetical objectives. First, there is the struggle to defend the artist's individual autonomy and maintain the distance from society that allows a critical perspective. But at the same time, there is the refusal to accept art's isolation from everyday life and a desire to overcome the institutional and status boundaries that maintain this separation. In the manner of his analysis of Manet's *Olympia,* Witkin offers an interpretation of a particular artwork that, for him, crystallizes a significant moment in aesthetic and social change. In this case, it is Latham's masticated *Greenberg.* Like all avant-garde gestures, this was a radical rejection of what came before. But it also represented a radical departure, rather than another oscillation between the two faces of modernism. The transition to pop art was also a transition to a higher level of abstraction—the "somatic"—in which the subject's own sensing is the object of perceptual attention. For Witkin, pop art invited a new mode of perception for the social formation of late capitalism that transformed both the objects of mass culture it was quoting and the subject viewing these quotations.

Stylistic transitions are also the focus of Julia Zhang's chapter, but in her case, it is in Chinese avant-garde art. Through a survey of representative artworks and interviews with members of the Chinese art world, Zhang identifies three stages in Chinese modernism. These stages coincide with critical junctures in Chinese political history: the first in the 1920s with the fear of colonization following the Opium war, the second in the 1970s at the height of Mao's era, and the third in the 1990s following the incident in Tiananmen Square. As Zhang shows, artists at each of these historical junctures used aesthetic means (artistic style) to interpret their historical moment and convey a desired vision of Chinese modernity. During the first two stages, Chinese modernity was defined in relation to a "West" that occupied the sacred side of the binary cultural code, representing the promise of scientific progress, freedom from political oppression through democracy, and the preservation of human rights. In the 1920s, the vision of modernity was expressed in the incorporation of Western "realist" style with ancient literati painting. In the 1970s, a different vision was expressed through the rejection of the state-sponsored artistic style, the overt political content of artworks, and the obvious allusion to Western avant-garde styles (such as futurism, dada, and surrealism.) But after 1989, the meaning of the "West" changed. As market liberalization took off and Chinese artists became increasingly dependent on Western buyers, the West became demystified. It came to be seen as the source of all that was profane about modernity—the decadence, moral degradation, greed, social alienation, and materialism. This view was expressed artistically through postmodern styles that celebrate irony, cynicism, and detachment or styles aiming purely to shock Western audiences through artistic explorations of violence. In Eyerman's terms, Zhang's analysis demonstrates how art can provide a cognitive space for the criticism of contemporary society, the articulation of a political project, and the imagination of a different future.

From the mythical constructions expressed in art, we go next to a consideration of the myth of the artist and the artist's subjective experience. Sherwood begins by reminding us that Durkheim's greatest insight in *The Elementary Forms of Religious Life* is that society and its institutions are permeated by a religious force. The social institution of art is no exception. If we accept Durkheim's spiritual model of society, then we must also accept the artist as a spiritual actor in two senses: first, as a "religious" actor (orienting to the sacred in terms of her motivation to create), and, second, as a collective representation of the sacred (as expressed through the ritual form of the artist biography.) Sherwood explores the "religious" dimension of art through heuristic models based on Durkheim's definition of the soul. The first is the *immanent* model where the soul is understood as a kind of energy or force. Using a phenomenological approach, Sherwood demonstrates how this model provides insight into the artist's creative process. Through excerpts from artists' writings, he shows that the artist's own experience of the creative power of the sacred can be both positive (as in the case of inspiration) and negative (as in the case of resistance.) The second is the *transcendent* model, where the soul is conceived as an ideal or higher external power. Using a hermeneutic approach, Sherwood shows how this model applies to the artist as a collective representation. With the examples of John Lennon and Andy Warhol, he demonstrates how the artist, as a historical and cultural figure, is the focus of ongoing imaginative construction. Controversies tend to erupt over "definitive" biographies of these artists not because of disputes over factual details but because they have become emblematic of society's moral authority. It is through ritual processes such as narrative that the collective conscience attempts to purify the image of the artist, restoring or imposing a "soul" in the immanent sense. Ultimately, Sherwood argues that the sociology of art has suffered from a lack of theoretical innovation and it is only through the reinterpretation of the classics that the field can be reinvigorated and new directions found for the empirical study of art and artists. By returning to classical theory, he is able to offer a more creative and more cultural approach for the investigation of subjective experience and the deeper elements of the collective imagination.

In the next essay, DeNora explores how the music of an art hero, Ludwig van Beethoven, was constructed as a "workspace" for the modeling of new conceptions of agency in early nineteenth-century Vienna. This discussion resonates with Eyerman's notion of art as a conceptual space. In contrast to her earlier work on Beethoven that emphasized the determinism of social structure, here DeNora traces the influence of scientific and philosophical ideas on musical critical discourse and musical performance. She shows that as music came to be understood as the medium par excellence of the sublime and the "inner life," the composer became reconfigured as a new kind of agent, a "master" of music who had power over musical materials and the ability to "mesmerize" the audience. It was during this cultural transition in Vienna that Beethoven emerged as a heroic figure. In the second section of the chapter, DeNora takes this analysis a step further, showing how discourses associated with Beethoven were embodied and elaborated through the performance of his piano music. In an important sense, Beethoven's body was inscribed in his music; it demanded a more visceral approach to the instrument through new techniques, postures, and physical choreography. These became the insignia of Beethoven's own genius and that of subsequent performers of his music. But not everyone could be cast as a Beethovenian performer. The physical and performative features required by Beethoven's works clashed with conventional standards of aristocratic composure and compromised feminine propriety. Beethoven's music provided an "object lesson" in how to be an agent in Viennese social life, but the modes of agency it modeled were not available for everyone. DeNora shows how the emerging gender segregation at the keyboard and the physical markers of musical genius were underpinned by notions from the "science" of physiognomy that was popular at the time. While some of these discourses have lost their cultural currency, the legacy of pianism as the vehicle for masculine display continues to pose a problem of performance for new generations of female pianists.

Providing further evidence of a performative turn, the last chapter in this volume outlines a new "performance perspective" for the sociology of music. Whereas previous sociological perspectives have approached music as an object either produced by an industry or used as a resource in social action, McCormick proposes an alternative orientation that approaches music as a mode of social performance. McCormick begins by articulating how the six elements of social performance theory (Alexander 2004) apply to the field of music. To demonstrate the analytical insight of this multidimensional approach for empirical research, she uses illustrative examples from the field of classical music to show the broad range of topics, musicological and sociological, that can be brought into the same framework and seen in a new light. McCormick then identifies the limitations of the production/consumption paradigm that can be transcended through the performance perspective. The first is the reduction of analysis to the element of social power typical of the production perspective. As a multidimensional approach, the performance perspective brings the dynamics of social power in proper relation to the other elements of performance. The second is the project of demystification and the systematic denial of meaning typical of the art worlds approach. By recognizing aesthetic action as meaningful and reconsidering sociology's divorce from the humanities, the performance perspective can investigate how aesthetic and social meaning is negotiated through the interaction of aesthetic form, enactment, and interpretation. Finally, the performance perspective can resolve the methodological individualism typical of phenomenological reception studies by addressing the broader cultural structures that shape aesthetic action and experience.

Our central aim in this book is the presentation of a sociology of the arts that takes meaning seriously. While any sociology of the arts must discuss art in society, meaning has become a secondary concern to social organization in this area of the discipline. Whether they speak about the production of culture or the construction of art worlds and fields, sociologists have been reluctant to address questions of value, interpretation, and experience, except with an eye toward debunking the claims of others. This has left us with an empirically vigorous, yet aesthetically lifeless, sociology of the arts. The essays in this volume have sought to point beyond production to new meaning-centered directions.

CHAPTER I

Toward a Meaningful Sociology of the Arts

Ron Eyerman

It means more, than it means to me.
—*G. K. Chesterton, on the meaning of poetry*

Art forces us to gaze into the horror of existence, yet without being turned to stone by the vision.
—*Nietzsche, on the birth of tragedy*

Hearing a classical piano concerto streaming from a window while sitting out in the courtyard of a large apartment complex, I was moved to speculate about the class, age, ethnicity, and gender of the person listening to it. It later struck me that I was suffering from an occupational hazard, that of the intellectualizing sociologist. I could just as well have enjoyed the music or tried to guess its composer or performer. I could have made judgments concerning the quality of the piece, of the performer. The point is that there are many ways of listening to music or viewing a work of art and also a professional division of labor dividing the various ways of approaching the arts along disciplinary lines, so that the sociology of the arts would concern itself with their social organization, while art history would address the art of various time periods and so on. Such differentiation and specialization has also been conceptualized in terms of "dimensions,"

13

as in a "sociological dimension" and an "aesthetic dimension" of art and artworks. From this perspective, the sociology of the arts is afforded sociological dimensions, such as "who is listening," and not aesthetic dimensions, such as "what does art mean, what is good or bad art," which is exactly the path I chose in my eavesdropping. (This essay is my own attempt to overcome this occupation hazard and to cross disciplinary boundaries by pointing in the direction of a meaningful sociology of the arts.)

One may speak about meaning in connection with the sociology of the arts in several ways. When it is considered at all, recent studies have focused on the production of meaning, on giving or imposing meaning. The process of meaning production, the attempt to evoke a desired response, as well as to communicate a designated message, has been studied from the perspective of semiotics as encoding. Influenced by Roland Barthes (1993) and others, studies have sought to uncover coded messages lodged in images and sounds as they are diffused through contemporary society. The process of encoding is described either as an unintended or intended process: the intention to make an object mean something in particular through representation. An artist or writer may intend to tell a story with a moral, didactic intent and thus to embed or encode that meaning in the story or painting; narrative religious art is an obvious example. Whether or not that aim is successful can be said to depend on an audience's ability to interpret or read the message in the intended way.

In discussions of a culture industry stemming from classical critical theory, the process of meaning making was studied through a synthesis of Marxian and Freudian ideas, which brought together notions of ideology and commodity fetishism, the cognitive and the emotional, the conscious and the unconscious. In the less normative, more explanatory vein of the contemporary production of culture, the process of giving meaning is studied from an organizational perspective as a commercially driven process. Meaning making is here entwined with marketing needs, with finding or creating an audience for a particular product, be that an automobile or a genre of popular music. This sort of meaning making has come to be called *branding*, highlighting the ideas and organizational decisions concerning design, manufacture, and promotion, which turns objects into desirable products through attributing meaning. "The Story of the Sony Walkman" (du Gay et al. 1997:13*ff.*) is an example of what is described as a "signifying practice" in the "production and circulation" of meaning.

Making meaning has also been a key phrase in the symbolic interactionist tradition in sociology. Erving Goffman (1972), for example, studied the making of meaning from a performative perspective, how actors attempt to transmit meaning through gestures as well as words, to define a situation by convincing others of its meaning. Goffman's ideas have been applied under the general rubric of "framing" to the struggle over meaning in discursive contests, as various individual and collective actors attempt to impose their definition, or meaning, of a situation onto others. The hermeneutic and semiotic traditions of textual analysis conceptualize meaning as embedded in texts or objects, where meaning is a matter of interpretative decoding, as much as encoding. Such meaning may be more or less consciously encoded, by artists or by a culture industry.

In other words, several approaches to meaning are available to a sociology of the arts. In conjunction with these, one can also speak of the social and historical meaning of the arts themselves: what art means in particular cultural and historical contexts. This brings attention to the idea that what we call art is first of all culturally and historically conditioned. Such conditioning can be said to occur on at least two levels, first in relation to the very idea of art, implying, for example, the creating of relatively useless objects made for expressive purposes only, as distinct from craft, where similar skills are involved in the making of useful objects. This historical development has been claimed as a distinctive one in Western culture. Second, given this distinction, what is included and what is excluded as "art," in the form of either an individual work or a more general technique, is also historically conditioned. Photography was first considered a craft largely because of the mechanics involved but also because of its military and commercial applications, but it has by now been assimilated into the world of art, just as filmmaking has.

One can also talk about the meaning of art from the perspective of why particular arts, conceived of meaningful expressions, arise and reappear at specific historical junctures (Danto 1997). The novel offers an example. Ian Watt (1957) connects the emergence of the novel to the rise of a new reading public, something that could be understood from the point of view of the production of culture; that is, a new audience, a new market, created the conditions for the emergence of a new artistic form. But Watt goes much deeper in arguing that this audience had interests of its own, an interest in self-knowledge. The new art form, in other words, spoke to, had meaning for, an audience it helped to constitute, aside from any commercial interests an author or publisher might have had. Social conditions important here were a rise in literacy, an increase in leisure time, and an interest in the subjective as well as objective world. As Watt discloses through a textual interpretation of three British novelists, the new literary genre told a story through the eyes of a unique yet generalizable individual, an everyman or everywoman, which was crucial to its appeal. As a distinctive genre, the novel captured emerging social relations and new possibilities of experience, even if such experience existed only as fantasy for the maid, the housewife, or the gentleman who read them. The world was changing, and the new art form, the novel, reflected those changes at the same time as it provided a means for experiencing and understanding them. The novel, in other words, meant something meaningful.

WHAT IS ART, AND DOES IT MEAN ANYTHING?

Definitions of art are notoriously difficult, and those interested in a thorough discussion of the alternatives may turn to Davies (1991) for a philosophical treatment and Shiner (2001) for a cultural history of the concept. Carroll (1998) thoroughly analyzes approaches to "mass art." Whether one is an analytic philosopher out to find necessary and sufficient conditions for defining art or a museum visitor wondering what makes this particular object "art," the idea of art is a contested concept. One thing is certain, however: how we think about and experience art is historically conditioned. The modern concept of art came into use in the 1400s; before then, there were similar practices that we today would identify as art, such as the making of images, but they were not understood as art, as aesthetic, but rather as relating to religion and to religious experience.

After centuries during which art was seen as craft, a skillful application of established conventions that ornamented useful objects or represented historical and religious narrative and important personalities, art achieved a degree of autonomy from its cultist and representative functions and from the guild and craft mentality that had previously defined its meaning and limited its development. A distinctive, separate space for the making and display of objects designated as art was put in place, which also provided the grounds for a new form of experience: the aesthetic. The idea of aesthetic experience—and, in its more utilitarian form, art appreciation—implied a form of contemplation and reflection separate from its earlier religious, cultist, ritualistic, and political forms of representation. It also implied a designation of social spaces and practices suited for that purpose, as art academies and museums were established. These provided material grounding for the ideal of art as a distinctive mode of experiencing and knowing the world. It was also the grounding of what came to be called an art world.

Accompanying this development was the notion that art and the aesthetic were something distinctive and separate from everyday life and its experience. In its original formulation in the eighteenth century, art was meant to stimulate reflective contemplation on the meaning of beauty. Once this separation was put in place and the distinctive meaning of art objectified in an aesthetic discourse and in the works themselves, once the autonomy of art was institutionalized in this way, these views could be contested and challenged, setting up a dynamic that has permeated and motivated developments in the arts ever since. Challenging this separation and the institution of art itself, according to Peter Burger (1984), was the defining characteristic of avant-garde movements in the early twentieth century.

The idea of an autonomous realm of art and its materialization in new institutions had an enormous impact on those who created and those who appreciated and viewed art. It has also underpinned the sociological study of the arts and the idea of a distinctive art world. Within the frame of an autonomous realm, the notion of the artist as a distinctive role and personality became possible. One of the classic works in the sociology of art, Norbert Elias's (1993) posthumously published study of Mozart, is a study of the effects of these changes on the composer. Tia DeNora's (1995) study of Beethoven, done from the production-of-culture perspective, attempts something similar. Once established, it became possible to study the distinctive behaviors, as well as the distinctive experiences, that developed and became associated with this social space, the field of art or the art world. The behaviorism and instrumentalism that has accompanied the sociological study of art worlds has provided us with insightful and often witty accounts of the posing and posturing that goes on within the walls of art galleries and museums.

Questions concerning what "art" means, in the double sense of what art is and what is art, are relative to time and place. This seems to be a truism today, but that view, too, is historically contingent. For in the unfolding of the history of art, one finds strong claims about universal meaning concerning what art is, and, in addition, what we call art today carries something of those earlier designations about its meaning. The same claims about the historical nature of the meaning of art can be applied to the meaning of the artist. Thinking of oneself as an artisan is different from thinking of oneself as an artist, and this difference affects the meaning attached to the practices involved in each.

In its historicity, art is an achievement concept (Kulka 1996:7), meaning that it carries inherent normative notions, which may vary and are open to challenge, but they still remain there. This point in fact is part of what is taught in art school, along with the various techniques of representation. In his study of how art is taught at American universities, Howard Singerman (1999:2) recalls his own formal training toward becoming an artist, noting that "it was clear to us that something historical was at stake in the name we took." For Singerman and his classmates, calling oneself an artist implied a burden of responsibility that made it both heavy and meaningful at the same time (see Sherwood, this volume). Contemporary discussions concerning the meaning of art and the role of the artist call forth previous discussions, just as any image—if the history of art be conceived of as the history of images—cannot be conceived in the absence of those images that precede it. Asking the question: "What does art mean?" is always done from some rooted point of view, rooted in time and place and in the particular location of the person asking the question—which at the same time recalls a sedimented discourse of posing and answering this question.

To repeat, one can take up the discussion about meaning and art in a number of ways: one can view art as a concept, an object, a practice, and an experience. As opposed to the ancient view, the modern perspective on aesthetic experience has focused on the individual. Without attempting an anachronistic return to a golden age, I think it both possible and fruitful to talk about a collective mode of aesthetic experience. When viewed this way, art can be said to open an imaginative space (individual and collective) from which to view the world and from there to represent it, through various media—paint, music, sculpture, film. This space can be material, as in a theater, a club, or a social or cultural movement, and imaginative, as well as collectively and/or individually experienced. It can also be collective in the sense that the history of art is as much a world of experience as it is of images and texts. Like experience and like tradition, art is at once historical and transcendent, reaching backward and forward, to past and future art spaces. It is also present. Writing about an American painter, for example, the art historian Stephen Polcari (in Joachimides and Rosenthal 1993:69) writes:

> Mitchell Siporin was a mainstream American artist in the 1930s. A true believer in the social purposes of art, he established himself as a painter of the "people." With paintings of the American scene, of the Haymarket worker's riots in Chicago, images of the homeless and subjects derived from social history, Siporin joined others in defining the imaginative space of the 1930s as pride in, and protest against, American life. By 1951 that imaginative space was gone. Instead it was an art of inwardness—virtually abstract canvases of dreamy, moody ambiguity and complexity.

Polcari here captures both the transcendent and particular nature of art as experience and imaginative space. The Great Depression restructured and refocused modernist styles in the arts, the optimistic and future-oriented focus on the pulse and magical power of machinery and urban life, with the socially oriented realism of the 1930s, with its focus on a lost but "usable past" and an uncertain future.

This latter way of viewing art as experiential space can be contrasted with the notion of an "art world" or a "field" of art, which also make use of a spatial metaphor. From this perspective, an art world or field is something one enters into, which then plays a determinant role over one's actions and beliefs. Though similar in ways, the perspective I am offering gives more place to imagination and creativity, as meaningful and constitutive of the space, rather than something external and determinant, a reified space one enters like a maze. Art, in other words, can provide a space within a space, a place from which to view the surrounding world yet not be untouched by it. It can be a collectively realized Archimedean point, not unlike that of theoretically driven science or an ideologically driven social movement. This perspective would not be unlike the idea of cognitive praxis (Eyerman and Jamison 1998), where art would be conceptualized as a form of social activity through which new kinds of social identities and practices emerge. In this sense, art is like any other social activity, a form of practical activity informed by some underlying project. What specifies and distinguishes art is the form and content of that project and the related practices. Art is a frame of reference in constant interaction with a social context. While all social activity is creative, art is defined by this self understanding. As a cognitive praxis, art is a space for individual and collective creation that can provide society with ideas, identities, and ideals. An imaginative space for the imagination, as well as an ascribed and conditioned social practice, as the production of culture perspective would have it. Like a social movement, art opens a space for experimentation, social and political as well as aesthetic.

Within this space, art becomes meaningful in different ways. Its meaning is contextual; and as context may shift, so, too, may meaning. The meaning of a work of art is determined neither by its creator nor by the conditions of its production. Meaning is created in social interaction, an interaction within a larger context. As Orlando Figes (2004) writes of the attempt by the composer Dimitry Shostakovich to explain the meaning of one of his symphonies,

> the Fifth Symphony is a good example because it reminds us that all "meaning" in music is constructed socially, and hence is never

stable, because it depends on the historical experience and associations of its listeners. What made the Fifth so highly charged with
subversive meaning was not so much the coded messages (which
no doubt went by largely unnoticed) as the public's awareness
that, in composing that symphony.... Shostakovich was fighting
for his life.

This example implies that although artworks may be open to multiple interpretation, all interpretations are themselves embedded in
meaning. There may be no one authentic reading or experiencing of
a work of art, but one central characteristic or meaning of art is that
it opens itself to and aims at creating a space for the experience of
and reflection on meaning.

More than experience and wider than the practice of making or
viewing artworks, art can be conceptualized as a means of approaching and knowing the world, as a cognitive as well as (per)formative
practice. In this sense, it is similar to the cognitive practice mentioned
earlier. Art can provide a means through which one can gain an understanding of the world and ones place in it. In *Music and Social
Movements* (1998), Andrew Jamison and I tried to show how musical
performance provided a sense of collective identity, a sense of belonging as well as an understating of the nature of reality and ones place in
it to social movement activists. While our examples were drawn largely
from popular culture, the idea of high art as a means of knowing was
central to the sociology of arts as practiced by Theodor Adorno and
the early Frankfurt School.

MEANING IN ART

Art tells the truth about society.

—*Adorno*

One of the central issues concerning a return to meaning in the
sociology of the arts is the question of any knowledge claims made
in forms of representation. How might knowledge be expressed and
communicated in artworks, how might such claims be received in
their public reception, and how might they be evaluated by more
distanced observers and analysts?

The production of culture has primarily conceptualized this matter within claims to authenticity, taste, and distinction, all of which
can be conceived with an instrumental view of culture, as fabrication
or as resource, part of a tool kit. On the other side, a long-standing

romantic and idealist tradition has preserved what today is rather disparagingly referred to as an essentialist notion of meaning. As Grana (1989:18) describes this tradition, it "at least since Hegel and in some respects earlier, [has] attributed to the creation of images the power to cause reality to stand and reveal itself before our eyes." I intend to carve out a middle ground between these positions.

Ancient thought recognized three modes of knowing—memory, art, and reason—while the Renaissance celebrated the role of art and the artist in prolonging memory through the painted image (Baxandall 1972). Our contemporary world has nearly succeeded in identifying knowledge with reason and reducing art to issues of taste, distinction, and money making. Rather than tracing this development (one can turn to Bernstein 1992 for such a study), I will take this reduction as reflecting something essential about the contemporary world. While primarily useful in analyzing the inherently meaningless products of mass consumption, the production of culture perspective can to some extent be usefully applied to obviously meaningful art, such as Holocaust poetry, folk music, or political art (see, e.g., Berezin 1994). Under the conditions of late or postmodernity, these, too, can at least in part be explained with reference to organizational forms and decisions, markets, reputation, and career paths. Although essential to any analysis of art in the contemporary world, this perspective leaves something essential out. Not only can it be faulted for denying the possibility of meaning embedded in artworks, mass produced or otherwise, and for not taking into account the possibility of varied reception of audiences, the production of culture cannot conceptualize art as a form of cognition and a realm of experience.

Ironically, it is Adorno, an originator of the "culture industry" and the production perspective on the arts, who provides the pathway to the return to meaning in the sociology of the arts. Despite the pessimistic outlook expressed throughout his work, most especially in *Dialectic of Enlightenment* (Horkheimer and Adorno 2002), Adorno's aesthetic theory and concrete analysis of artworks reveal how artistic expressions might pierce and shatter the reified world created through culture industry.[1] Adorno suggests that while mass-mediated popular culture affirms established power relations in both totalitarian and liberal regimes, a truly dialectical artistic creation, Schoenberg's compositions, for example, can penetrate and help deconstruct this reified world. This is not the place for yet another exegesis of Adorno's aesthetic theory—many excellent presentations are available (e.g., Witkin 1998; De Nora 2003) in addition to the often dense original works themselves (Adorno 1992, 1997, 2002). Beyond Hegel and Marx, Adorno returns to the ancient linking of art with cognition, to the "truth-bearing" potential in all art forms. He encourages us to view art, even "mass art," as a way of approaching as well as representing the world. This does not exclude the possibility that art distorts cognition, producing false consciousness, which is of course the viewpoint put forward in *Dialectic of Enlightenment* (Eyerman 1981). Entertaining the opposite perspective, however, opens the possibility that art might also teach us something about ourselves and the world we inhabit, more even than the class position or status aspirations that the production of culture claims to uncover. This places meaning at the center of any sociology of the arts. Art becomes a conveyer of meaning, a form of communication, with the potential for enlightening as well distorting. Rather than merely reflecting the social conditions of its production, art may provide a prism through which to reflect on those conditions.

As a form of meaningful communication, art encourages response. Artistic expressions can be characterized by the intention to engage the observer, to form a relation and create a connection. It is as much form as content that is important here. We expect and anticipate art to be meaningful. "What is that supposed to mean?" is a phrase often evoked by a work of art. Meaning is thus fundamental to art itself and so, too, to the self-understanding of the artist. The actual content of an art object and performance embodies meaning, in that it communicates an encoded message, consciously intended as in narrative and realist art—which may or may not be successfully received—or more vaguely as mood or sensation, as in abstract and performance art and wordless music. Adorno's focus on artistic form, rather than specific or intended contents, reveals the interactive basis of meaning in art. For him, meaning emerges in the performance (McCormick, this volume), the interaction among performer, work, and audience. This implies that meaning is not simply a matter of intention or embedded code (the subject matter of art criticism, biography, autobiography, and hermeneutics generally) but a relational interaction. As such, meaning is emergent, the subject matter for a relational and communicative approach to understanding.

While one may analyze the meaning potential, or, as Stuart Hall (1980) puts it, the "preferred" reading, embedded in an artistic expression, how this preference or potential is actualized should be studied as an interactional process. As Hall suggests, while individual artists or even a culture industry may intentionally or unconsciously encode an art work with a preferred meaning, that work must be received, interpreted, decoded. Audiences may vary and be various, thus finding different meanings in the same work or performance. In fact, the same work/performance may be experienced and interpreted differently at different times by the same person at a different stage of life or through a different interpretative framework. One can apply the framework provided by the production of culture and that of critical theory and arrive at a different interpretation.

Adorno was concerned with the fact that the products of a culture industry were manufactured for effect—that is, to evoke a familiar and comforting response. This was also the basis of his criticism of some works of "classical" music: that these compositions were not only so familiar as to be canonized, but also that they could "encourage the listener to give in to familiar pleasures and patterns," as DeNora (2003:153) puts it. What is significant here is the idea that interpretation and reception are essential to any discussion of meaning in art and, equally important, that reception is conditioned by frameworks already in place of interpretation, the "'familiar pleasures and patterns" referred to earlier. It is this conception of art that leads Adorno to prize Schoenberg over Stravinsky. In Adorno's interpretation, Schoenberg's music is intended to jolt reception out of those familiar patterns, to shock the listener and evoke reflection, even if it evokes a feeling of revulsion. One immediate problem, of course, is that not many listeners last long enough to entertain that possibility. The same may be said of any avant-garde work. My point is primarily that meaning is fundamental to art and should also be in any sociology of the arts and not that Adorno was correct in his judgments.

Rather than debating the general question of what art is, Adorno advises us to begin in the concrete, with what is currently called art, finding there a sedimentation of all that has been previously called art. His point is that identifying something as art, whether through the intentions of the creator or its placement in an "art world," signifies not only an actual object but a tradition of expressive activity, of embodied and embedded meaning. In the particular experiencing of some thing called art, we recall a more universal form of human experience, a way of relating as well as expressing and creating, which we know as "art." We recall through this object a tradition whose fundamental basis rests in the attempt to represent what is essentially unrepresentable—namely, the human spirit. A similar point is made by Hans Georg Gadamer (1987) when he writes concerning aesthetic consciousness, "Here one does not simply look beyond what one sees ... but dwells on it.... The mode of being of what is observed 'aesthetically' is not presence-at-hand" (82).

A particular art object is always more than its material appearance; it points not only beyond itself to a tradition of objects, sounds, images, and practices but also to something beyond the material. This quality, however, may not be immediately apparent in the experience of a particular artwork. Each particular experience awakens only a possibility, offers a potential or suggested reading in a more positive sense than that suggested by Hall, which must be completed with the aid of critical reflection, in order to fully appreciate its meaning as art. This is why, according to Adorno, one needs aesthetic theory, a critical discourse, to "complete" the work of art, to point us beyond what appears before us, to what has been and what could be. The term *aesthetics* was invented (by Baumgarten) "to supplement 'logic' by providing a science of sensitive cognition and the arts" (McKeon 1972:45). The concept was meant to capture the unique sensation derived from the experience of art. Immediate, aesthetic experience could be deepened, Adorno thought, through the critical reflection spurred through dialogue with engaged others. An artist and a work may speak for themselves, but what they say and what an observer experiences can be deepened through a many-sided dialogue. As Willem de Kooning (whose painting will be discussed later) put it, "There's no way of looking at a work of art by itself. It's not self-evident—it needs a history, it needs a lot of talking about, it is part of a whole man's life" (quoted in Stevens and Swan 2004: 000).

While part of a long-standing tradition, what is characteristic of art produced under the conditions of modernity, where art has gained a relative autonomy from religious and political power, is its sense of its own authority. Art under modernity, modern art, carries its own legitimation. The culture industry both reinforces and alters this. Art that has no legitimacy beyond itself is defenseless against the laws of the market. Under these conditions, art is also limitless, as many artworks as possible can be produced; the only limits lie in the capacities of the producers and consumers. This capability is both liberating and debilitating, free from religious and political control; art is purposeless and from the perspective of authority, meaningless. Thus, it is open to many forms of "outside" interpretation and manipulation.

Beyond communication, art's only purpose is to express and represent, and herein lies art's critical potential. Real art in Adorno's estimation re-presents a totality, a whole, even as fragment. This totality, an accomplished work, evokes response and interpretation as it presents itself to an audience. Modernity is an age of fragmentation and alienation in which pro-offered wholeness can evoke contentment, a nostalgia for a bygone era offering solace, or it can evoke critical reflection on the fragmentation and its causes. Yet, at the same time, it is the whole/fragment, this particular artwork, that reminds us of the totality that is art. Who decides which of these is forthcoming? It is not given. It cannot simply be the task of the critic, for the response to an artwork cannot be entirely known a priori, since response implies reception. At best, the critic can reflect on the potential contained in works of art and offer criteria or prediction as to what response might be and with whom, which audience. Even if one can say, like Adorno, that artistic truth is a form of sensuous (of the senses and emotions) truth, as contrasted with conceptual truth, a form of truth that balances concept and intuition, a critic can only postulate what response an artwork might evoke in an audience. The dialogue is an ongoing process, never entirely complete, among artwork, critical discourse, and current audience.

Let me illustrate this point with the example of the painting *Excavation* created in 1950 by Willem de Kooning, as it is analyzed by his biographers (Stevens and Swan 2004):

> For decades the art of painting had seesawed between expressionist impulses and classical reserve, between the rational and the irrational. In particular, cubism and surrealism presented two contrasting alternatives, one depending upon geometry and the grid, the other upon the looser form of dreams. *Excavation* was a magisterial synthesis of these two claims on modern truth.... de Kooning gave this synthesis a strongly American character. *Excavation* had none of the monkish reserve of Parisian cubism, but seemed brash and pulsing, like a blinking sign in New York. A black and white city that glinted with occasional color, New York was itself a kind of synthesis of cubism and surrealism, a combination of strict grids and liberating gestures in which order and chaos, reserve and craziness, appeared locked in tense balance.... No other American painting ... conveyed with comparable force the jazzy syncopation of the city.... Modern culture is often the study of fragments and lost wholes. An artist, to bring that study powerfully to life, must remember the whole the way that shard remembers the pot. In *Excavation,* something perfectly complete seemed to have shattered, but de Kooning had recast the pieces into something worthwhile. Not once in *Excavation* did the brushstroke seem to forget the larger composition. The picture pieced together the fragmentary, the broken, and the partially concealed. De Kooning's refusal to abandon the pieces—and the past—was what fundamentally distinguished *Excavation* from Pollack's work, the parts were subservient to the "all-over" image. His art left the past behind and rose above the quarrel between cubism and surrealism; it was a transcendent art. But de Kooning still composed a picture so that the gritty individual details mattered, they did not completely submit to the larger idea. De Kooning refused to transcend or escape the self in any larger sense. A self was too hard won, and too prized, especially for an immigrant. (295–97)

I've quoted this analysis at length to reveal what one could mean by "truth" concerning a work of art and also to exemplify the type of thick description one finds in the best art criticism. Here we can see some of the essential components of a meaningful sociology of the arts: a focus on the artwork and the artist while placing both against a complex historical background that includes the artist's biography, the history of art, and the current social situation. Artwork and artist are here related to social and cultural structures, the urban scene and the modern experience aesthetically interpreted within a long-standing tradition of the visual arts.

This can be usefully compared to the analysis offered by Diana Crane (1987) of the American avant-garde in the same period. An advocate of the production of culture perspective, Crane explains the stylistic changes both leading to and within the "New York Art World, 1940–1985" (the subtitle of her book), primarily with reference to the expanding market for artistic products, the number of interested galleries, the career opportunities and changing role of the artist, as well as the internal structure of networks for the production, display, and consumption of art. The artworks themselves are hardly considered, except in illustration, and de Kooning is mentioned only as exemplifying the link between art and craft and for his leadership position among avant-garde artists. *Excavation* is not mentioned at all. While impressive, Crane's study is hampered by its focus on external factors in explaining development in the arts. If she were correct, one would expect that a key figure in her art world such as de Kooning would have adapted and adjusted his painting style to a changing art market. What happened was actually the opposite. For example, although some well-positioned actors in the New York art world gave *Excavation* the nod of recognition, and although it was selected to represent the United States at the Venice Biennale and for display at New York's Museum of Modern Art, it was not sold until much later. If it were correct that markets and other institutional mechanisms were the forces driving artistic change, then de Kooning would have produced more abstracts in the same style to follow up on this modest success. Again to the contrary, the artist shifted gears back to figurative representation, despite the loud proclamations of gatekeepers such as Clement Greenberg that such forms were dead. Gatekeepers were certainly important in turning public attention to the new art and in providing space for display, but it was the artists, as individuals and as a self-aware collective, that drove this great historical shift. They did it in the face of great opposition, not for money or because of markets but because art meant something.

As the living combination of a European tradition of painting and the consummate New Yorker, de Kooning articulated a truth in his work about the modern urban experience. "Truth" here relates to a way of picturing the contemporary urban experience, in a way that captures, makes apparent, its basic structures. It is a truth that is made available through the actions/gestures of the artists and that is recognizable, not necessarily to everyone but certainly to those who open themselves to the aesthetic and to the surrounding critical discourse. To say a painting requires patient reading and critical reflection is not much different than saying the same thing about a classical text in sociology. One must open oneself to any truth/knowledge it discloses and be prepared and predisposed to see it.

This interpretive notion of truth in art can be compared with the representational notion propounded by Pierre Bourdieu. Bourdieu (1996) argues that one can take a text, a "good" novel, as truthful representation of an emergent structural change. Reading Flaubert's *L'éducation sentimentale* in the light of his own grand sociological theory, Bourdieu uncovers a new field of artistic production in formation through the actions of the individuals described in the novel and the author who produced it. The best novels, Bourdieu argues, are not simply fictions that emerge from nowhere into the heads of geniuses; rather, they are representations of those invisible forces we like to call structures, which help shape human thoughts and actions. The sociological reading of Flaubert, then, aims at making visible the otherwise invisible conditions of human action, including those that shape the author and the work itself. Furthermore, Bourdieu believes that some aspects of social structures are better grasped through novels than the more direct methods of scientific research. This is the case because putting on the mask of fiction or storytelling permits writers—as well as their informants—to reveal things that otherwise might go unsaid or unnoticed. The novel, in other words, can give voice to worlds, as well as processes, that we would rather not see or speak about. Through the mask of fiction, one can say and uncover the truth.

There are two levels to this truth in fiction. The first is the more conscious one of an author who is permitted to say things in fictionalized form that he or she might not be permitted or willing to say openly. Satirists from Molière to Mary MacCarthy found it more convenient to describe the social relations of their time and place in semificticious form. There is less chance of losing friends and creating enemies in this way. The second concerns the way less conscious things may be revealed to readers, in the same or different time and place than the author, about the social constraints that shape them.

These are the "rules of art" referred to in the title: the logic that writers and literary institutions obey and that express themselves in submerged form in and through their works. These structures form the basis of the literary field on which authors are placed like strategic actors and that shape the form and content of their writings. The way of approaching truth in literature is limited by a reflective theory of truth and a lack of concern with the meaning of art beyond what it may say about society. It proposes that both literature and author are determined by the social conditions in which they are produced. Good art and the great artist provide sociology with a mirror, rather than a prism, to look through; it is an instrument rather than a meaningful activity.

ART AND POLITICS

One could put the question "Does art mean anything?" to a minister of culture in a totalitarian regime. Plato advised against the introduction of new musical genres, because he thought any change in musical convention would lead to a change in society. Why, in the 1960s, did the Spanish dictator Franco close the film school in Madrid? The answer is that totalitarian regimes, like reductionist theories, usually apply either a reflective theory of meaning, where meaning is thought to lie in an object, a person, or an event, or an intentional theory of meaning, where meaning is something a speaker, author, or artist imposes through representation. Any society seeking to dictate the content of the lives of its citizens takes forms of artistic expression very seriously. One need only look at the organized attempts to censor and control those who create and produce art. But censorship like art is difficult to define (see Korpe 2004) and is present in some form in all societies, even those that view art as a leisure activity for the sophisticated and wealthy few, and censorship is only part of the issue. Totalitarian regimes or leaders view the arts as vital forms of social integration and as expressing, and teaching, the basic values they seek to impose. That is why the arts must be monitored and controlled, and that is why they are meaningful. For such regimes, art that is valued for its playful, individual expression can only be a threat; it does not have to be especially political in its theme or content. In repressive regimes, the arts can become an underground for subversive activities, which is why Franco closed the Madrid film school and why in the more liberal period after his death film became an explosive force of creative expression. In such a context, even Hollywood films can serve as the basis for rebellion and critical reflection.

It is not only totalitarian regimes that give great attention to the meaning of the arts. Liberal societies take notice of the arts when they expose or transgress deeply rooted values. More than this, however, the arts are essential to myth making, and myths are essential to any form of collective identity, especially if we give credence to Gramsci's view of myth as "a concrete phantasy which acts on a dispersed and scattered people to arouse and organize its collective will" (quoted in Taylor 1997:30). The power of art to rouse the emotions or to uplift, educate, and distinguish has been a common view of many individuals and governments. The arts have played a significant role in the struggle for recognition, for individuals and groups, as well as nations. They have been important in the grounding and maintenance of national identities; the foundation of national academies of art and national museums are examples.

Images were important in constructing the United States from the very beginning. The silversmith Paul Revere's engraved image of the massacre by British soldiers of unarmed American colonists in Boston in 1770 was a powerful weapon in preparing both the armed rebellion and the new collective identity. After the successful revolution, John Trumbull, the son of the governor of Connecticut, wrote to President Thomas Jefferson explaining why he undertook to create a series of paintings depicting the revolutionary struggle:

> The greatest motives I had or have for engaging in, or for continuing my pursuit of painting, has been the wish of commemorating the great events of our country's revolution. I am fully sensible that the profession, as it is generally practiced, is frivolous, little useful to society, and unworthy of a man who has talents for more serious pursuits. But, to preserve and diffuse the memory of the noblest series of action which have ever presented themselves in the history of man: to give the present and future sons of oppression and misfortune, such glorious lessons of their rights, and of the spirit which they should assert and support them, and even to transmit to their descendents, the personal resemblance of those who have been the great actors in those illustrious scenes, were objects which give a dignity to the profession, peculiar to my situation. (quoted in Pohl 2002:78–79)

With these words, writes Pohl, "Trumbull not only sets out the patriotic nature of his artistic enterprise, but also argues for the political significance of history painting for the new nation" (79). Sentiments such as these must certainly have a place in the sociological analysis of the context in which these works of art were created.

As opposed to Revere's engravings, there was no commercial market for Trumbull's paintings, and the museums and other sites for the representation of a national culture were yet to be built. The genre in which he painted his heroic imagery was still associated with the hated British and thus not valued in American homes. Perhaps this is an easy example, but it does reveal that a market is itself a meaningful construction, even when there is money to spend and people willing to spend it.

The opening of a national gallery is often seen as a sign of cultured maturity, as is the presentation of artists who represent it. Many regarded the founding of the Municipal Gallery of Modern Art in Dublin in 1908 (Herrero 2005) as a significant and necessary step to national recognition and independence, just as the opening of the National Academy of Design in 1865 and the Metropolitan Museum of Art five years later was intended to raise the status of New York City to the level of Paris and London (Whelan 1995). Minorities within nations have also viewed the arts as means to proving themselves worthy of recognition and citizenship, as the struggles of many minorities in the United States have shown. For American blacks, one of the first steps toward overcoming the stigma of slavery was the objectification of cultural competence through literature and other forms of art. Representations of an African American experience in literature and music were central ingredients in the formation of a new collective identity, something that helped contest the negative stereotypes presented in the dominant culture (Eyerman 2002).

Arthur Danto (1997) provides a different sort of example of the role of the arts in national prestige: the trust and reconciliation shown in allowing former enemies access to exhibit works from another nation's collection. "After World War II, the official exhibition of national treasures was a standard gesture through which a nation expressed to another that hostilities were over, and that it could be trusted with objects of inestimable value" (23). Even for nations without such treasure, the holding of an international exhibition on its soil can be used to announce a newcomer or the return of an ousted nation to the world community: "no sooner had apartheid ended in South Africa than Johannesburg announced its first [biennial], inviting the governments of the world to sponsor exhibitions in acknowledgment of its moral acceptability" (23).

For new nations and for those within them, the arts often have an important symbolic value. The creation of a distinctively American art was, for example, an important national project in the late nineteenth and early twentieth centuries. As part of an even wider project of creating a distinctly American culture, it was one that engaged many individual and collective actors as well as various forms of expression and schools and styles within them. Cultural institutions and entrepreneurs, such as the photographer Alfred Stieglitz, were an important part of this project, and the role of distinction and gatekeepers should not be underplayed. But, to follow that example, Stieglitz was also someone who identified himself as an artist, not an artisan or businessman. For him, aesthetic and moral criteria were central to his missionary approach to art, and the American art he sought to promote had to be the best art done by Americans, by which he meant a distinctive form of modernism. Like Adorno, Stieglitz believed that good art could be identified by its internal qualities, as well more superficial stylistic features. He also believed in the enlightening and reflective qualities of the experience of art and that the role of an exhibition (e.g., the famous Amory exhibition of 1913) was not to promote an artist, even less to make money, but to educate the public and to influence the practicing artist on the real meaning of art.

The arts have also been seen as important for the cultivation of local populations, increasing and promoting moral health and a sense of common humanity (Nussbaum 1995). While it is possible to dismiss these aims as false consciousness or as smokescreens for real economic interests or status seeking, this would surely be a limited, if not distorted, picture of a complex process. One could dismiss the views of John Trumbull quoted earlier as hopelessly old-fashioned and confine them to the dustbin of history, but that approach, I believe, also would be closing the door too soon on the possibility that art might really mean something even to the most professionalized and jaded commercial artist. A sociology of the arts should take into account the meaning of art for an artist, the biographical and historical contexts in which intentions and motivation were articulated and their effect on the artwork created. It should place an artwork in its contemporary context as well as in the context of the history of art. This is a lot to ask and to strive for, and it may not be possible in every case to complete, but as a regulating ideal it will serve for a richer and deeper sociology of the arts.

TOWARD A MEANINGFUL SOCIOLOGY OF THE ARTS

If we are to move in the direction suggested in this chapter and in the introduction, we need to consider the following steps toward a meaningful sociology of the arts:

1. Shift from a paradigm of production to one in which creation and imagination are central components, to an interactionist, nonmechanistic model of imagining and experiencing, as well as making, where meaning is conceptualized as an emergent property in the interaction between subject and object.

2. Adopt a noninstrumental conception of culture. Culture should be conceptualized as a relatively autonomous space of expression and knowledge, and art as a relatively autonomous space of experience as well as practice. Art may then be seen in relation to the wider culture of an age, as well as a long-standing tradition that affects the acts of creating and making. From the relatively autonomous space of art, one can view society, as well as viewing art from a societal perspective. We can learn about society through art, as well as learning about art through society. A noninstrumental view would also permit us to put culture back into history and to view culture historically. This approach would broaden the view of art beyond the notion of an art world or field—that is, a distinctive relatively autonomous social space to include distinctive experience, expression, and transgression. Such a move would not necessitate a return to the routinely criticized view of music or painting as high art, some pristine activity. Rather, art could still be studied as a socially constituted cultural form, yet with distinctive characteristics, one of which is a powerful dose of meaning and significance, which can be embedded, embodied, and transmitted over time and space.

3. Bring the artwork and the artist back into view. This perspective would allow that there is something more to art than production for distinction, status, class, or power. It would allow inclusion of the expressive element, a bringing forth, an aspect of meaning, for the creator and for the audience. Doing this is not meant as a project of reenchantment, a return to a mythological, romantic view of the artist, but to recognize that there is something that distinguishes art, even when considered from the point of view of an institutionalized social practice, that transcends or escapes commodity production. Art may be a commodity, but its distinguishing feature is its being embedded in meaning and its ability to evoke a distinctive, aesthetic response. Such emotional response is distinctive in its being unique to the experience of art.

4. Shift to a perspective that includes collective as well as individual actors. This view would mean moving from masters to movements and beyond the producer/receiver (production/reception) dichotomy to a performative approach (see McCormick, this volume) that includes both sides in a communicative interrelation and

also opens up for notions of script and repertoire, to preexisting cultural codes and conventions on both sides. Here we can learn from Adorno and from Alexander (2004). Performance moves us through meaning and interpretation to action, to acting and acting out. It complements narrative and textual analysis, as performance turns texts into practice. Internalized rules and conventions, as well as narrative frames, guide performative actions. This turns attention to preformed modes, scripting, coded messages, and framed responses. Yet, within all this, something new emerges, on the side of both creation and reception, permitting emergent possibilities. Performance emphasizes corporality, being there, doing, viewing, and experiencing.[2]

This chapter has aimed at being more than merely programmatic, however. More than these concluding steps, I hope my discussion and illustrative examples have revealed the fruitfulness of a meaningful sociology of the arts. If not, the following chapters will surely do that.

NOTES

1. When drawing parallels to classical critical theory, it is important to keep in mind that Horkheimer and Adorno conceptualized the notion of a "cultural industry from the point of view of a theory of social change, looking at "culture" from the perspective of a potentiality for reflection and change. They were movement (critical) rather than traditional (academic) intellectuals. They were not designing a sociological research program, at least not in the first instance, and they rejected the academic division of labor as an imposition on critical thought. They also rejected the idea, inherent in the production of culture/art world perspective, that one needs to carve out a distinctly "sociological" approach to art, to find a niche in the academy. From their perspective, one of the most meaningful aspects of art was precisely a potentiality for critical reflection. This was the basis of their ideology critique and the meaning of their notion of a culture industry.

2. We can also gain from a look at Maffesoli's (1996) argument about postmodern neotribes (see also Oliva 2002). Against a focus on individuality and the Bourdieuian notion of class habitus, Maffesoli argues that new collectivities are transitory and performative. This turns attention to more transient and transitory subcultures around consumption and aesthetics than to fixed individual or class-related characteristics or strategies. The idea of tribes or more temporary and transitory movements is also directed against the classical conception of subculture developed in cultural studies, which was more structural and stable. Maffesoli's notion also embodies a sociality, which is neither functional nor rational instrumental, more about being

and playing together, more imaginative and creative, than instrumental or status or class oriented. It develops the notion of aesthetic aura, where aesthetics refers to a feeling, experiencing. While the notion of aura is familiar from the work of Walter Benjamin, here one gets the feeling and sense of being together, a sociality, as opposed to Benjamin's more subjective, individual-oriented usage. Through a collective experience of aesthetic aura, a nonidentical community, a nonconservative community, is created, based on a shared meaningful experience rather some essential common base, in race, class, or gender, for example. This is a form of community that moves beyond the "tyranny of meaning" (Barthes 1977:185). Within the aesthetic, the nonidentical relationship between the self and sociality is illuminated: "aesthetics is a way of feeling in common. It is also a means of recognizing ourselves" (Maffesoli 1996:77). From the novel onward, popular culture has given the modern individual a new source of reflection on the self, an aesthetic reflection, that can see oneself and one's class or group in a new light and offer possibilities for change. Mass culture, in contrast, implies manipulation, not creativity or possibility. Aesthetics is about communication and pleasure, about self and other, and about experience and sociality, not merely a discourse on the beautiful. This would also permit moving within and beyond the textual focus on meaning.

CHAPTER 2

Chewing on Clement Greenberg

Abstraction and the Two Faces of Modernism

Robert W. Witkin

In the creative turmoil that is unleashed within social movements, modes of cultural action are redefined and given new meaning as sources of collective identity. For brief, intensive moments, the habitual behaviour and underlying values of society are thrown open for debate and reflection, and, as the movements fade from the political center, their cultural effects seep into the social lifeblood in often unintended and circuitous ways.
—*Ron Eyerman and Andrew Jameson,*
Music and Social Movements

Artistic avant-gardes are invariably referred to as "movements." As Poggioli (1968) argued in *The Theory of the Avant-Garde,* these networks of artists, poets, critics, and intellectuals behave like social movements rather than "schools" of art. Each new avant-garde justifies itself with a critical rhetoric concerning moral and political issues—how to live as well as how to make art. The skills of poets are often deployed in supplying the plethora of words that surrounds the production of new

35

art. They announce a relationship to modern society, a philosophy of life and an active disposition with respect to art and culture. As Poggioli noted, an estrangement from society, from both tradition and convention, has been key to the formation of avant-gardes. The very marginality of art in the modern world, its lack of an acknowledged social function, did more than anything to provoke the intensity with which avant-garde artists addressed the "alienation" of the subject. The marginality of the artist with respect to the social formation and the alienation of the subject were linked phenomena. Theodor Adorno once remarked that it matters little whether we understand art. What is important, he argued, was that art understands us; as part of that, he meant that art understands the alienation and marginalization of the subject in modern society. It was Adorno, too, who advanced the knowledge claim of art, insisting that the arts tell the truth about society more than do documents.

Establishing the linkage among social, semiotic, and aesthetic systems is key to understanding the contribution that the aesthetic dimension—always broader than art—makes to social formation. The focal point of my chapter is a particular transition between avant-gardes that took place in the 1960s. Sociologists have always liked watersheds, and I want to explore briefly, from a sociological point of view, the meaning of the break with abstract expressionism represented by the advent of pop art (I am not ignoring the complementary development of minimalist art in this period, but to include it here would require a much longer chapter). There was always a tension between two different objectives in modernist art. I shall call them the "two faces of modernism." On the one hand, artists reacted against the special status of art and everything that kept art isolated from everyday life. They sought to extend the embrace of the aesthetic to the world of ordinary everyday things, making anything and everything equally worthy of aesthetic attention. On the other hand, artists sought to defend the autonomy of the artist as "individual," as holding a distance from the world and as taking up a critical position in relation to it. These tendencies were incompatible; they pointed in opposed directions. The tension between them, I argue, gave a special impetus to the development of avant-garde movements.

The radical submersion of art in life, which was one pole of aesthetic modernism, threatened to extinguish the special status and autonomy of the artist as individual and, with that, the power of expression and the function of modern art as critique. Correspondingly, the pursuit of a defense of the artist as individual and of self-expression as both critique of society and self-understanding—the other pole of aesthetic modernism—demanded an ascetic withdrawal of art from involvement in the world, an intense formalism that contrasted strongly with the drive of artists to immerse themselves and their art in everyday reality. The emergence of pop art in the 1960s asserted the claims of a radical submersion of art in life against the reigning avant-garde, abstract expressionism; the latter instantiated the defense of the individual and of self-expression. The transition that is the focus of this chapter thus illustrates the tension between these two faces of modernism.

I shall seek to anchor my observations concerning the emergence of modernist avant-gardes in a line of reasoning about the development of abstraction in art that I originally introduced in my 1995 book *Art and Social Structure* and that I have since developed further (Witkin 2005).

LATHAM'S "HAPPENING"

It is commonly accepted that the earliest self-conscious manifestations of pop art appeared in England in the 1950s. The British artist Richard Hamilton, famous for his creation of a poster entitled "Just What Is It That Makes Today's Homes So Attractive, So Appealing?" probably coined the label "pop art," although the term was actually popularized in an article by Lawrence Alloway. By reputation, however, it is the American artists associated with pop art, most notably Andy Warhol, who are held to be the most important contributors to the movement.

John Latham, an English artist, well-known in the avant-garde circles of the time, specialized in the 1950s and 1960s in the production of reliefs that involved subjecting books to various kinds and degrees of destruction, including mutilation and burning. In the mid-1960s he lectured at St. Martins College of Art in London. Although not really classifiable as a pop artist, Latham was closely associated with many of the individuals who were. Both Richard Hamilton and Lawrence Alloway, as leading members of the group known as the "Independents," had written introductions to exhibitions of Latham's works. He is perhaps best known for creating a notorious assemblage consisting of a leather case containing letters, the remains of a book from which several pages had been torn out, and several labeled vials full of powders and liquids. This strange collection of objects can be seen both as a part of a sustained program of artworks centered on the book as an object and, if taken in isolation, as an avant-garde gesture of Duchampian magnitude. To make it, Latham borrowed a book, widely used by his own students, from the college library.

He took it to his apartment and, tearing out several pages, fed them to one of his "students" who slowly chewed, masticated, and spat out the residue into a bowl. Latham then added yeast and sugars to the "critical cud" produced by the digestive juices of the student and sometime later poured the fermented liquid into glass vials. A month or so after this, the college library sent him an overdue notice for the book he had borrowed. In response, he delivered to them the fermented residue in the glass vials. Eventually the whole assembly was acquired by a New York museum. It was exhibited together with a letter from the authorities at St. Martins College of Art and Design, dismissing Latham from his teaching post. If the college was outraged or offended by the meaning of Latham's gesture, it was not the reason given for his dismissal. He was officially dismissed for the crime of having willfully destroyed college property—namely, a library book entitled *Art and Culture* by Clement Greenberg.

Gesture art such as the exhibiting of Duchamp's urinal or Latham's masticated Greenberg appears at key moments in the formation of avant-gardes. The gesture is simple and stark, rich in its implicit meanings, in its heralding and encapsulating of a change that is already under way, in this case, a reconfiguring of the relationship between Art and Culture. I have no idea whether the choice of that particular title was significant for Latham, but I imagine it was. He might have chosen other titles by Greenberg, but this one seems particularly apposite. Certainly the choice of Clement Greenberg himself as the author to be chewed up here was quite deliberate. Greenberg, as the most important American art critic of the twentieth century, was the authority who had formulated and defended a project for modern art that had enjoyed widespread approval among the cognoscenti. He had championed the art of the abstract expressionists, clearly one of the major art movements of the twentieth century, seeing in it the very epitome of the ideal of modern art that he had set out in his major theoretical papers. Greenberg was himself art trained and a painter, and his ideas on art developed in dialogue and personal friendship with many of the major artists of the century whose work he championed. It was their work that provided the exalted exemplars of modern art for postwar artists in Britain and the United States. However, notwithstanding the admiration that many of the sixties artists felt for the work of Jackson Pollock, Mark Rothko, Barnett Newman, Clifford Styl, or Willem DeKooning, they were, themselves, striking out in what appeared to be an altogether different direction. Latham's alchemical distillation of Greenberg as the champion of an earlier avant-garde, like all avant-garde gestures, marked a difference, a departure, and it did so in the most decisive manner. Latham may also have been commenting, wittily, on the great importance attached, by artists and art colleges, to the written word, to critics as authorities; and to be suggesting that it is what artists actually do, and not what critics say, that determines the direction and significance of new art.

We are confronted here with one of those radical breaks or discontinuities in which artists strike out in a way that does not appear to follow on from what has gone before, that constitutes a radical "critique" of what has gone before. Such a discontinuity is a defining characteristic of an avant-garde movement. Greenberg came to exemplify, for many of these sixties artists, a vision of modern art that had to be rejected. Latham's gesture was not an isolated critical statement. During the period of contemporary and so-called postmodern art, rejection of Greenberg became fashionable enough to justify the invention of a term for it—"Clem-bashing." It was not one-way hostility, either. Greenberg disapproved strongly of the new art in this period, not only pop art but also minimalism and postmodern art generally. Greenberg had his disciples, and they, too, took issue with the new art. The response of the minimalist artist Donald Judd, for example, to the critique of minimalism by the Greenbergian critic, Michael Freid, was marked by a harshness of language bordering on contempt; acrimony has frequently characterized the tone of these debates.

Although Greenberg's writings were voluminous throughout a long career, the heart of the position for which he is best known was developed in three papers (Greenberg 1939). They offer a perspective on the evolution of modern art and of modernism; they present a theory concerning the critical project of avant-garde movements of art; finally, they polarize serious modern art and the production of mass cultural art that Greenberg labeled "kitsch." To many, the ideas that Greenberg developed in these papers still constitute a significant contribution to making sense of the profound changes in art that first appeared in the second half of the nineteenth century in the paintings of Manet and Cézanne.

The rejection of the mass culture of modern urban societies was key to this development. Greenberg's famous 1938 paper "Avant-Garde and Kitsch" set up this polarity. The same conditions in late capitalist society, to which the modernist avant-gardes were a response, gave rise also to mass culture. If serious art was essentially a radical critique of art, its capacity to hold its distance from society was bound up with its resistance to contamination from the mass-market art produced by the modern culture industries. Mass culture was placed under the sign of mass manipulation. There was nothing progressive about it, according to Greenberg. Kitsch obtained its material from the residues of now-defunct art. It sustained neither the individual nor self-expression. It consisted in market-tested effects to be worked on individuals. The opposition of modern art to modern mass culture was a keystone of Greenberg's theorizing and a vital part of his program for defending "individualism and self-expression" under modern conditions.

Adorno and Horkheimer published *Dialectic of Enlightenment* in 1947 (see Horkheimer and Adorno 1986), nearly ten years after Greenberg had published his paper "Avant-Garde and Kitsch." In it they set out their now-famous ideas about the culture industry. However, some six years earlier than Greenberg, Adorno had set out a similar position in his 1932 paper "On the Social Situation of Music" (see Adorno 1978). The resonances between Greenberg's polarization of serious and mass art and that of Adorno (and Horkheimer) are very clear. Moreover, Adorno, like Greenberg, makes this tension integral to sustaining the individual and the power of expression in a world set to extinguish both. Both thinkers were concerned to resist the sublation of serious art in what they perceived to be a moraine of mass cultural kitsch. It is this latter possibility that threatened to expunge the autonomy of the artist and the possibility of his or her maintaining a critical distance from society, from the status quo.

Greenberg contrasted the social situation of modern artists with that of the artists who preceded them. Artists working in earlier times under the patronage of princely houses, wealthy citizens, or the church, did so in conditions in which art was charged with social responsibilities and social significance. The emergence of the artist in the nineteenth century as an autonomous own-account worker, free to create at will and to sell his creations in the art market, coincided with a loss of social functions and the loss of a determined location within the institutional structures of everyday life. It coincided, that is, with the virtual exile of art from the world of socially significant or socially important work. As part of this change, artists no longer had a meaningful subject matter; they were no longer the professional visualizers of the holy stories, nor were they charged with realizing aesthetically the great cultural themes that bind a community. As Theodor Adorno and, later, Peter Burger argued, the attainment of autonomy status for the institution of art was also the mark of its irrelevance, its lack of a meaningful location in the praxis of everyday life. Nevertheless, even when art had been stripped of its former relationship to society, art continued to be made that presupposed all the old social functions to be intact. At the time that Manet produced his modernist art, the majority of artists continued to make art as if the society that that art addressed had not already passed away, having been supplanted by a late capitalist world in which these older forms of address and of representation were false and no longer possessed truth-value for the times in which they were made.

For Greenberg, the mark of responsibility for modern artists was to dedicate art to ridding itself of the residues of the former relationship to society that still encumbered aesthetic practice. Modern avant-garde art, in Greenberg's thesis, undertook this task through mounting a rigorous critique of art itself. Modernist art, he argued, took art's own methods for content, subjecting them to a continuous process of refinement and purification in which everything nonessential and external to artistic practice was progressively eliminated. This process had to be achieved separately for all the arts, Greenberg reasoned; the requirements of critique were specific to each medium. Greenberg's insistence on the refinement and essential specialization of each of the arts led him, therefore, to devalue all notions of an integration or merging of different arts.

Painting was the art that was of primary interest to Greenberg. Modernist painting ceased to simulate the three dimensions of sculptural space. It shut down the deep space of pictures preventing the observer from visually entering the picture. It was a process begun with the paintings of Manet and Cézanne. Painting shared certain attributes in common with other arts. It shared color with both sculpture and theater and it shared the supporting frame of the picture with the (proscenium arch) theater; the flatness of the picture plane, however, was unique to painting as an art, and it became more or less fundamental in modernist painting. For Greenberg, the pursuit of flatness in modern art represented the most sustained drive toward the purification of painting, its self-liberation from all nonessential, nonartistic residues. In addition to freeing itself of any obligation to simulate the three-dimensional space of sculpture, painting renounced any obligation to represent or reference an external reality. Painting always has a content, claimed Greenberg, but it has no essential need of a "subject matter." The modern artist retreated, argued Greenberg, to the ground of purely artistic means; that is, to a practice that was very much narrower in its compass than had formerly been the case but a practice that left the artist more securely in control of ever more powerful means of expression.

This retreat to a formal level of aesthetic practice was an endorsement and program for "abstraction" as the essence of a truly modern art; that is, the artist's use of color, light, line, and form in purely expressive ways, freed of the obligation to represent something. What, then, is the pay-off for this journey into abstraction? For Greenberg, the journey of modernist art is clearly perceived as an intensification and heightening of the self-understanding and self-possession of the artist as an individual. The very category "individual" posits an entity with some degree of distance and "independence" from the world to which he or she must relate. The individual's journey of self-understanding was clearly conserved in all this; thus, Barnett Newman observed in 1948 of himself and of his fellow abstract expressionists, "Instead of making *cathedrals* out of Christ, man, or 'life,' we are making [them] out of ourselves, out of our own feelings" (Newman 1992).

The artistic movements of the sixties ran directly counter to what were seen as the maxims of Greenberg's ideology of art and as the principles governing the practice of much modernist art. They represented the opposing face of modernism. Greenberg's belief that serious art should hold its distance from mass culture, that the latter should be seen as the enemy of serious art, was rejected by these artists who launched themselves in the opposite direction, embracing mass culture in all its aspects. Greenberg's ascetic program for art as the self-critique of art was condemned by his detractors as a recipe for an essentialist formalism that isolated art from the world. Finally, Greenberg's attempt to secure a safe haven for the artist as individual and for the ideal of art as self-expression was also rejected. The way back into the world for pop artists consisted in overcoming this type of differentiation. They insisted on the destruction of hierarchy and embraced a new and more "democratic" universalism, declaring all things to be *equally* worthy of attention from an aesthetic standpoint and refusing to privilege the individual, who was the very foundation of previous aesthetic hierarchies. The attitude of these artists was broadly cool, witty, open, and objective rather than critical. Paintings became filled with recognizable objects from soup cans, Coke bottles, and Brillo boxes to cars, advertising images, consumer goods of all kinds, as well as famous people. The figural realism of depictions appeared to reject the commitment to modernist abstraction. Like the Dadaists before them, pop artists sought to subvert the claims of Art that were buttressed by critics such as Greenberg. It was precisely those claims that had exiled art from the praxis of everyday life.

ABSTRACTION

Greenberg linked the abstraction of modern art directly to the self-critique of art, to its purification and refinement through art's withdrawing to a ground that was purely artistic. It was a process that reflected the situation of art in modern society. To most people, however, abstraction describes art that departs from perceptual-realism, from the simulation of the optical values that would be obtained in natural perception. In other words, abstraction is popularly seen as painting that either distorts or dispenses with the real appearances of things. Such a conception is quite inadequate to define abstraction and results in a number of anomalies. The majority of the world's art would, on that definition, have to be described as abstract; abstract art would then include both the art of archaic and primitive societies as well as that of modern industrial societies. Perceptual-realist art, on the other hand, has appeared in very few places, notably classical Greece and Rome and in Europe from the late fourteenth to the late nineteenth centuries. It was only ever perfected in the European case. We would then be suggesting that the flat formal art that preceded the Renaissance was more abstract than the Renaissance art that followed it or the Roman art that preceded it. Such a view effectively robs the concept of abstraction of any real analytical value in relating the formation of artworks to the social formation. There is a need to rethink the problem of abstraction as it applies to art and to society.

PERCEPTUAL MODES

Because a work of art is an organization of the perceptual and is only able to organize the body of the subject in and through sensuous means, perceptual relations and perceptual truths determine what kind of organization of the body (here, equivalent to an "understanding") is possible and, therefore, what kind of organization of social and cultural values can be realized in a work of art. In our everyday perceptual relations, different sensory modalities are involved together and are mutually confirming. We see with our eyes what we grasp with our hands, for example. The *contact values* yielded through grasping and touching objects are visually reinforced by the *distal values* yielded in seeing those same objects at a distance. These, in turn, should be distinguished from the *proximal values* that make up the purely visual qualities—color, texture, shape—values that are "closest" to the eye as a sensory system. Thus, a visual scene may be resolved into recognizable objects and figures that can be "handled" (yielding contact values), seen at a distance (yielding distal values), and sensuously apprehended as a patterning of shapes and colors, of visual qualities (yielding proximal values).

At a perceptual level, the lowest level of abstraction consists in the *haptic* mode; dealing with the world at the level of its "contact values." At that level the individual cannot decenter from what is immediately within his or her grasp, cannot gain distance or a view of the whole. In the *optic* mode, by contrast, the individual has an overview, can grasp the world at a distance and insert reality into the organized system of (optical) appearances that constitutes a point of view. Finally, the highest level of abstraction is reached in what I term the *somatic* mode, in the sensuous patterning of visual qualities that captures not the object as such (the object of contact values) or the object as seen (the object of distal values) but the seeing of the object seen (the object of proximal values); the subject at this level of abstraction takes his or her own sensing as the object of perceptual attention.

Each mode affords unique possibilities for aesthetic ideation and its appropriation by artists in a given type of society is secured by its affordance of these possibilities. The fact that the process of picturing is visual does not mean that it centers itself on an optical mode of perception. The ancient Egyptian artists adopted a mode of picturing that appropriated the possibilities of a haptic mode of perception; that is, they sought to depict real things in their completeness and not the appearances of things. An archaic Egyptian figure is painted as a composite of frontal and profile views and proportioned in accordance with what are held to be essential metrical relations. To the extent that art appropriates a haptic mode of perception—that is, deals with the world at the level of contact values—it is "thinking" values at a relatively low level of abstraction. Those values must be carried in the depiction of the outer form itself and cannot be made visible in the interactions among forms. The saintliness of saints or the majesty of kings must be made fully visible in the exterior of the form itself. The king may be depicted as very much larger than his enemies as though his majesty and superiority was a matter of absolute value and therefore visible in the attributes of his depicted person—in this case his size. Figures in such art do not acquire their values interactively. They are not relative but absolute values. In van Eyck's fifteenth-century painting of the *Virgin in the Church,* the church is rendered more or less realistically in its size-distance ratios, but the figure of the Virgin is gigantic relative to her surroundings. Arnold Hauser viewed art that obeyed nonnaturalistic rules of this kind as the art of aristocratic and hieratic societies, those in which social order was imposed from above and was not subject to the individuals ordered by it. Hauser contrasted this situation with that of bourgeois societies with developed middle classes, commercial enterprise, and a high degree of individuation. Such societies valorized the individual's point of view and depicted the world as it appeared from a point of view (i.e., from a distance). Bourgeois societies tend to democratic forms of government and universalistic systems of law. The development of such social formations became decisive at the time of the Renaissance and the revolution that occurred in the arts at that time can be seen as a raising of the level of abstraction at which the emerging city formations could think their most important values.

Renaissance artists appropriated the possibilities of an optic perceptual mode based on distal values, inserting the object into an organized system of interactional relationships. Consider the case of a perceptual-realist painting, one that successfully simulates a three-dimensional reality on a two-dimensional surface, allowing the receiver to see the frame as a kind of window through which a scene may be viewed, much as one might view a scene in real life. A perceptual-realist art clearly alters the structural possibilities for representing figures and objects and the relations among them in important ways. For example, to the extent that the space depicted simulates a real optical space and figures and objects are represented *as they appear from a particular point of view,* the attributes of depicted figures and of objects will be determined by the system of optical transformations into which they enter. No figure in such art comes complete and self-contained in its visual values, as it does in archaic art. Rather, the optical values that describe a figure are functionally relative and are determined by the figure's position and relations within a larger system of transformations relative to the assumed point of view of an observer (e.g., the figure varies in size and distinctness depending on its position; all such perceived dimensions are a function of the total system of relations in which the figure participates). This represents, in my argument, a raising of the level of abstraction at which values may be represented and, therefore, thought.

Modern artists have grounded aesthetic process in a somatic mode of perception based on proximal values and have made the "seeing of things seen" into an object of aesthetic attention. The sustained and systematic undermining of the optical coherence of visual representations, carried out by artists such as Picasso, at the turn of the twentieth century, was no perverse attempt to experiment for the sake of it or to worship novelty or contradiction. If objects and figures in such paintings became subject to massive deformation and fragmentation, it was perhaps less a statement about the object *as such* (the object of archaic art) or even the object *as seen* (the object of Renaissance art) as it was an exploration of the *seeing* of the object—that is, an exploration of the constitutive process through which sensuous perceptual relations are made. This paradigm shift involved a quantum leap in the level of abstraction. With cubism, the elements of aesthetic experience, color, tone, line, and plane were divided from one another and given new functions. They ceased to serve the demands of the distal object and moved over to meet those of the somatic subject. Color, light, shade, and line came to describe the *experiencing* of things rather than things as experienced. Color became a language of expression in itself. Tonality became a free rhythmic element in the construction of pictorial space. Line was freed from its role in describing the ordinary distanced objects of perception and became both a means of expression and a means of constituting a new spatiality, a new type of "object." Depth was renounced, and the picture plane, together with the purely pictorial business of painting, was made central.

At the somatic level of perception, the perceptual system attains a degree of autonomy as a locus of ordering and is no longer *embedded* in the world of objects. This growing autonomy of the perceptual process is identified, semiotically, with the growing autonomy of the signifier (as distinct from the signified) and sociologically with the emergence of a subject-centered locus of ordering in social relations. Relations among elements in a haptic space are *coactional*; in an optic space, *interactional*; in a somatic space, *intra-actional*. The movement to a somatic level of perception is movement to the most subject-centered mode of organization. This has nothing to do with becoming egoistic or unsocial. Rather, it is a claim concerning the level of abstraction at which social experience is ordered, a level at which meanings are fully relativistic and in which all foundational forms are subject to an "ironizing" vision.

ABSTRACTION AND SOCIAL FORMATION IN LATE CAPITALIST SOCIETIES

In Renaissance art, the construction of a truly optical space provides a constitutive ground for the interpretation of every fragmentary appearance of a thing. Thus, when a figure is seen from one position in one of its aspects, all the other positions and aspects that constitute the full reality of the figure—its plenitude as a visual thing—are present and active in determining what is perceived. We "see" a whole cup even when most of it is hidden from view. The third dimension is clearly important as a device or means for signifying this plenitude in the object or figure. Roundly modeled objects exist in a three-dimensional space. While only one aspect may be seen, the promise of all the other aspects making up the plenitude of the object is indicated in the projection of this continuous three-dimensional space. Objects and figures are perceived as being *in* space; their continuity is presupposed. This, in my argument, is a prerequisite for a medium charged with representing biographical and historical trajectories, with realizing an identity between the formation of individual biographies and the formation of society such that the intrapersonal and intra-actional life of the sensuous subject finds itself reflected in the interactional order that constitutes what Hegel called "the world's course."

It is precisely this (ideological) identity between individual and society that was challenged in modernist art from the middle of the nineteenth century. The new art increasingly withdrew from the interactional world to the intra-actional, subject-centered domain, to the arising of the world in the perceiving body of the subject. That is, art moved to a higher level of abstraction, to what I have labeled a somatic level. In literature the change was reflected in the transition from an object-centered realism to a subject-centered naturalism, a transition that can be seen in the development of the novel from the huge realist canvas of Balzac to the stream-of-consciousness writing that characterized the novels of James Joyce and of Virginia Woolf, or in visual art from history painting to the art of the impressionists, a journey in both cases that took art away from a dialectical temporality and emphasized the spatializing and present-centered aspect of experience. Late capitalist society, with its giant corporations, bureaucracies, extended chains of dependencies, the Taylorist microdivision of labor, and the development of mass culture, consumption, and advertising, belied an ideology founded on the primacy of the individual and on his or her supposed identity with a social order that is presumed to be the outcome of social interaction among the individuals who are its members; a social order that remains open and responsive to those members.

THE FIRST MODERNIST STRATEGY

While this shift in the locus of order in art from the interactional to the intra-actional was integral to modernism, there were, as I have suggested, two antithetical avant-garde strategies that coexisted within modernism. One strategy was to pursue the Enlightenment concept of the artist as "autonomous individual" achieving self-understanding and self-realization through expression but to do so in the light of the impossibility of achieving this within the compass of a bourgeois order. The response of the modernist artist, consistent with Greenberg's programmatic analysis, was to withdraw from bourgeois conventions to the ground of a pure aesthetic practice. The strategy was always problematic, however. The domain of intrasubjective experience, which provided a new locus of order, required that aesthetic practice define itself through expression. In the modern world, it could do so only through its resistance to and nonidentity with conventional bourgeois society.

The intrasubjective constitution of the subject could no longer be taken for granted, however. It is sourced and renewed through continuous engagement with the world and with new experience; if it is not, it atrophies in the hermetically sealed condition that describes schizophrenia; a condition that R. D. Laing called "shutupness." Art could attempt to secure its continued sourcing through a (negatively) dialectical relationship to society—that is, through taking the oppressive forces of modern society into itself and expressing the life process that had been mutilated by them. Writers such as Kafka and Beckett come into this category. Adorno's aesthetics of music champions such a solution. It is essentially a formalist strategy that seeks to retain the level of abstraction characteristic of the formation of bourgeois societies, a level of abstraction in which subject and object still tango together but in a relationship of nonidentity.

In a second version of this same modernist strategy, artists have sought to dive below or beneath the conventional bourgeois order, to engage the "unconscious" or the prebourgeois or "primitive" consciousness as though it were somehow possible to undo the ego and everything that has been put together by the division of labor, in order to reach a "state of nature" uncontaminated by bourgeois relations. Artists from Wagner and Stravinsky to the surrealists and, later, the abstract expressionists have sought to access the realms of both the primitive and the unconscious as if the realms of the primitive and the unconscious could substitute for the world in sourcing a vision.

However, both versions of this strategy were more or less assiduous in avoiding the resort to the material of mass culture, to the imagery, colors, and forms of advertising or the commercial world. When they did engage with this material, it was in an ironizing way. The continued survival of the individual in a world in which it was otherwise homeless demanded a rigorous ascetic restraint in respect of mass cultural art.

THE SECOND MODERNIST STRATEGY

The aim of the second modernist strategy, in contrast to the first, has been to overcome the separation between art and life; that is—to use Peter Burger's (1984) phrase, to secure art's reentry into "the praxis of everyday life," an aim that provides the second string to modernism's bow. Burger's principal exemplar of avant-garde art was the art of the Dadaists. Dada artists, in their use of "found objects" and in their challenge to the boundary dividing art from nonart could be seen as oriented toward art's return from exile to the praxis of everyday life. The anti-Art strategies of these artists jettisoned both the elitist claims of Art as well as those that reinforced the expressive individualism of artists. Not surprisingly, pop artists have also been referred to, on occasion, as "neo-Dadaists."

The distinction between reality and ideology, between art and society, so important to the concepts of the individual and expression, was effectively eroded by the advance of mass culture, which consumed reality to the point of standing in for it. With the collapse of reality into art and ideology, the very ground of the distinction between individual and world is undermined. This accounts for the dialectical tension between the two great modernist strategies. The preservation of the individual as the distillation of Enlightenment freedom and autonomy could not survive the embrace of mass culture. Equally, the destruction of the line that divided art from life was incompatible with both the institution of Art itself, as the fortress of an Enlightenment project, and the privileging of the individual and of self-expression.

Yet, there is reason to see this particular break, occurring in the 1960s, as especially significant from the point of view of "art and culture" (the latter phrase is the title of the book by Greenberg that Latham destroyed). The transition between abstract expressionism and pop art did not simply rerun the oscillation between the two faces of modernism. Rather, it shifted the ground to a higher level of abstraction and brought into play a new dialectical tension, represented, then, by pop art and minimalism. This raising of the level of abstraction consisted in the shift of the locus of order from the interactional "world as seen" to the intra-actional "seeing of the world." It is in and through its "seeings" that the re-formation of sensibility occurs and, with that re-formation, a changed relationship to the world. Pop art may have filled paintings with the colors, forms, and images of mass culture and advertising, but it was never a simple reproduction of these images. If it was, the reproduction of an advertising image or a product label might be expected to work on us much as the originals do and that is not the case. The images of the Brillo box, the Coke bottle, the comic strip, or the publicity photograph of Marilyn Monroe do not function in pop art as their originals do in everyday life. These "quotation images" might best be described as realizing "seeings" and therefore as appropriating what was meant to work on us, to manipulate us, as material for the realization of what we now actively form—namely, our seeings of things seen. With every such realization of a seeing, the sensibility of the subject is *re-formed.* Not only is the subject changed by this art of visual quotation, but so, too, is the world that is quoted. The more activated the subject at the level of seeing, the more does the world of media and mass culture have to engage with that activity. The originals appropriated as material for the formation of seeings will no longer work as they once did for those exposed to this appropriation. Both the sensibility of the age as well as mass culture itself is changed by this process. John Latham's distillation of masticated Greenberg in the decade of pop art, minimalism, and the Beatles may also have served to announce the raising of the level of abstraction at which social life is organized from an interactional to an intra-actional level. Abstract expressionism and Adorno's aesthetics have one thing in common: Both seek to preserve the individual and with it an interactional (albeit negatively interactional) relationship to society as part of the defense of the individual and of the Enlightenment project. The emergence of pop art and postmodernism should then be seen as a raising of the level of abstraction to the point where the locus of social relations is intra-actional rather than interactional and where all foundational forms are subject to an ironizing vision.

NOTE

The author thanks the Leverhulme Trust for its support of the writing of this chapter through the award of a Major Research Fellowship.

CHAPTER 3

The Meaning of Style

Postmodernism, Demystification, and Dissonance in Post-Tiananmen Chinese Avant-Garde Art

Julia Chi Zhang

Chinese avant-garde[1] art occupies an uneasy place in both domestic and global arenas of cultural production. This art emerged and developed under the crossfire of an authoritarian socialist state and an unappreciative domestic audience in the late 1970s, and in the 1980s, it finally established itself as a form of "unofficial art" that strived to be both politically dissident and formalistically transgressive. In the 1990s, China's pace of market liberalization and internationalization has become drastically accelerated. Interestingly enough, during the same historical epoch of a little more than one decade, the stylistic orientations of the Chinese avant-garde have gone through profound transformations. The previously politically committed dissident Chinese avant-garde art that emphasized formalistic purity or political disobedience has been transformed into a different kind of avant-garde that now actively collaborates with the Western art world and celebrates a new set of "postmodern" aesthetics. Playful pastiche, whimsical juxtaposition, and political irreverence have be-

51

come prevalent, and previous metanarratives deployed in the art of the 1980s are increasingly jettisoned.

The year 1989 is a significant turning point for Chinese avant-garde art because it was the year of the Tiananmen student movement, which changed the political climate of China from relatively liberal (prodemocratic) in the late 1980s to highly authoritarian in the early 1990s. Also, after 1989, China's marketization deepened at an exponential rate. Around the mid-1990s, China became fully integrated in the global economy. The high tide of capitalism had finally arrived.

This chapter examines the social and cultural meaning of the stylistic shift in Chinese avant-garde art before and after 1989, as well as various significant structural transitions that took place in the art world during the time. The discussion aims to account for the symbolic as well as material basis for the stylistic shift, with special focuses on two important mechanisms: (1) the mission of Chinese artists in both eras to use artistic style (socialist realism, Western modernism, postmodernism) as a meaning-laden medium to convey their particular vision of Chinese modernity—namely, how the West, as an artistic signifier and symbolic resource, has been understood and appropriated by the artists in their works; and (2) the structural transformations that have taken place in the avant-garde art world, especially the post-1989 hypercommercialization brought about by China's marketization and Chinese artists' accelerated integration into the international art market in the 1990s. Finally, the inevitable rise of a "discourse of authenticity" is discussed as a result of these two mechanisms.

THE SOCIAL MEANING OF THE "MODERN" STYLE IN CHINA

Chinese avant-garde as an artistic and social movement[2] emerged during the third-wave Chinese modernism[3] in art that emerged in the late 1970s, almost a half century away from the insurgence of the first-wave Chinese modernism initiated by painters Xu Beihong, Liu Haisu, and Lin Fengmian in the early twentieth century.

As harbingers of early Chinese modernism, Xu, Liu, and Lin each struggled with different alternatives in rendering unique artistic styles to create their art. The decision over style was crucial to them precisely because the creation of an unprecedented "Chinese modern" style in painting—more specifically, the decision over how much of a traditional Chinese style to retain and how much of a Western style to adopt—was highly sensitized and emotionally charged because of its social and symbolic implications. The artists' heightened imperative to appropriate a characteristically Chinese modern style is not hard to understand if we take into consideration the historical conditions in which they were situated: China at the turn of the century was plagued by tremendous domestic social unrest and encroaching colonization by Western imperial powers. By the 1920s, China had lost the Opium War to the British in 1840 and had signed a series of unequal treaties with various Western powers permitting them to build concession districts in mainland Chinese cities exclusively for foreign use, an action perceived by many Chinese as a great humiliation. Because of the specific political and historical conditions in which modernism took root in China, the constantly shifting modern style in China implied far more than a merely aesthetic decision. In other words, the modern style in Chinese art, from the very inception of China's modernization project, has been a key signifier of national autonomy and Chinese modernity.

As art critic Gao Minglu (1991a) puts it, "The history of Chinese modern art is a history of incessant conflict and fusion between traditional Chinese literati painting and paintings that inclined to adopt Western style." Gao acutely detected the "sudden loss of confidence" among Chinese painters over their centuries-old literati tradition at the end of the Opium War; however, he does not reveal the real source of tension over the modern style in China. The formulation of the "right" amount of "Westernness" and "Chineseness" in the Chinese modernist style reflects a deep-seated anxiety or desire for Chinese artists to signal their artistic break from tradition as well as their particular vision for a new Chinese modernity. Interestingly, despite their different backgrounds and divergent aesthetic and theoretical agendas, Xu, Liu, and Lin eventually unanimously settled on the idea that the art of their time ought to stay in a realm "between figurative and non-figurative" ("似与不似之间"). This stylistic decision is extremely important for understanding modern styles in Chinese art. Chinese modern artists saw realist, figurative, and photographic rendering of techniques with scientific three-dimensional perspectives in painting as a uniquely Western practice. The style itself is a gesture that the artist accepts values or ideas that have been imported from the West. Chinese modern artists' insistence on incorporating characteristically Western "realist" style, technique, and training (Xu was trained in France[4]) into Chinese modern art echoed a strong advocacy for positivism in the political and intellectual arena of their time, a tendency to use Western science and technology to help build a strong modern China (西学中用).

The second-wave Chinese modernism in art emerged during the high Mao years[5] when the realm of cultural production was strictly regimented by the state apparatus. The only legitimate, officially sanctioned aesthetic style of that era had been the socialist realist and the neotraditionalist styles, both serving a double function as political propaganda.[6] The socialist realist style was both technically and thematically "modern" and "Western," which was encouraged by the state mostly as a result of China's eager emulation of Soviet Russia at the time. The Russian socialist realist style in all the arts and literature was eagerly sought after by the official artists in China.[7] State-sanctioned socialist realism was also established in opposition to the abstraction-oriented "Western modernist" style that had become mainstream modern art in Western Europe and the United States for almost a half century. The Western "modernist" style was symbolically associated with the "evil axis" of Western democratic countries, the political rivals of China and the Soviet Union during the Cold War. Western "modernism" was condemned by the Chinese state cultural bureau as technically deficient and morally bankrupt; however, the distinctly "Western" socialist realist style was hailed as evidence that socialist China was actively modernizing itself and enjoying a certain artistic affinity with its socialist allies in Eastern Europe. According to Gao Minglu (1995), former editor at the Chinese official art journal *Art* ("Mei Shu"), the homogenized socialist realist style put great emphasis on a painting's "sleek surface" and "theatrical illumination," supposedly appealing to the proletarians. The stylistic qualities of this line of works earned itself a cynical alias: "the Red, Bright, and Illuminous" (红光亮). In this sense, socialist realism was also a reaction against the Chinese literati tradition, which emphasized aristocratic nonchalance and an elevated intellectual taste for merely grasping the meaning of the subject rather than the form ("Hui Yi 会意").

When the Chinese avant-garde appeared and demanded a voice, socialist China had just gone through some of its worst political nightmares. Millions had died during the Three-Year Starvation in the early sixties. A generation of young people's youth and prospects for education were decimated through the "sent-down" movement as well as incessant domestic upheavals and political purging during the Cultural Revolution. The relentless refurbishing and reappropriation of the rhetoric of class struggle during various political movements created a great cultural divide within the nation. At the end of the Cultural Revolution in the mid-1970s, China was at its political and economic deep end.[8]

The Pre-1989 Avant-Garde: The Continuation of Metanarrative Conflated with a Learned Western Modernism

We observe the third-wave Chinese modernism in art through the body of works that emerged in the late 1970s and were self-identified by the artists themselves as the "Chinese avant-garde." This avant-garde art movement started as a collective effort by a group of dissident artists, art students, and a few reform-minded critics and editors at several key art journals, exemplified by the official party art journal *Art* (美术) in the late 1970s, at the end of the high Mao era.

Avant-garde, translated into Chinese as "Qian (front) Wei (guard)," is a French term deliberately appropriated by this group of Chinese experimental artists to pay homage to their forerunners in Western modernism. Their choice of style was in opposition to the official socialist realist style but, more important, also the symbolic referent of it. It was a conscious choice that involved a great deal of risk.

Because of the subversive political message and formalistically transgressive style of avant-garde works, the pre-1989 exhibitions were constantly shut down by the state. The most significant event in the pre-1989 avant-garde movement was the China/Avant-Garde Exhibition that opened in the Chinese National Art Gallery in Beijing on February 5, 1989. A collective effort by avant-garde artists and curators, it exhibited 296 works by 186 artists. The exhibition was shut down three hours after its opening, when artists Xiao Lu and Tang Song decided to convert their installation into a piece of performance art by opening fire with a real pistol on their installation piece.

There was almost no solid audience base for the avant-garde art in the 1970s and 1980s. Most of the people who did show interest to this art were fellow artists, students, and progressive intellectuals who did not entirely agree with the Communist Party line.

Avant-garde art in China was first created by members of the amateur Star Group in the late 1970s. Stylistically, their style was identifiably "modernist" in the Western sense, which makes it relatively easy for us to distinguish them from the official and popular realists of the time. The pre-1989 avant-garde artists strived to incorporate more contemporary mediums such as installation and performance art in addition to regular oil painting. Unlike the émigré Chinese painters such as Chen Yifei, who made hefty sums producing commercially successful representational figure paintings of attractive young Chinese women for the international market in the 1980s (mostly for the wealthy Chinese patrons in the expatriate community), the pre-1989 avant-gardes had a truly international perspective aesthetically. They drew their stylistic imagination from the Western modernist canon from futurism to surrealism to Dada, which were made more accessible to some of the most ferociously curious and inquisitive students in the newly reestablished Chinese art institutions after 1979 when China officially reopened its door to the West (personal communication with artist Zhang Hongtu, December 2004). We observe strong "modernist" language in these pre-1989 works, as shown in Gengjian Yi's deliberate flattening of three-dimensional space and human body; Wang Guangyi's geometrical distortion and codification of a socialist propaganda image (figure 3.1); Zhang Peili's obsessively rationalistic deconstruction of a pair of clinical gloves (figure 3.2) (gloves have the symbolic reference to blood and actions of cleansing, purging, and violence in Chinese culture); or Wu Shanzhuan's 1988 installation piece *Painted over Rocks* (figure 3.3), a synthesized symbolic feast containing combined local and international referents: the red paint on the rocks immediately evoke images of ominous propaganda posters made during the Cultural Revolution, and the technique of paint splashing on the rocks was clearly influenced by German/American expressionism. In other words, despite the self-conscious "modernist" style in Wu's work that was Western in nature, the subject matter of these pre-1989 avant-garde art works was clearly rooted in Chinese history and especially the experiences of the Cultural Revolution.

It is not an overstatement to say that, at the end of the 1970s, the dichotomy between the realist versus modernist styles in Chinese modern art signified the two opposing alternatives of modernization projects for China, perceived by the Chinese artists and intellectuals of the time: dehumanizing, irrational, decaying Chinese socialism versus humane, rational, vivacious Western democracy. For the avant-garde artists, the "Chinese" and "Western" alternatives were placed, respectively, on the opposite symbolic poles of sacred and profane.

The idea of the West, immediately evoking positive symbolic connotations such as freedom, democracy, individual rights, human dignity, liberated sexuality, and romantic love, was consciously and unconsciously sought after and idealized by the avant-garde artists. To render this idealization aesthetically, they faced a necessary and inevitable aesthetic choice: realism or abstraction? For the 1970s Chinese avant-garde, the realist style appropriated by the conformist official artists and upheld by the orthodox socialist art academy had appeared increasingly trite and symbolically contaminated (by decades of propaganda art that stifled artistic autonomy). The avant-garde artists in the late 1970s and 1980s, longing for a radical break

Fig. 3.1. Wang Guangyi, *Mao Zedong No.1* (detail), oil on canvas, 1988. Photo by the author; courtesy of the artist.

from both the aesthetic and the social realities of their time, made a conscious, almost inevitable choice. They turned toward Western modernism, considering socialist realism, or realism of any kind, as a symbolically inadequate or obsolete signifier for the kind of Chinese modernity they envisioned.

The unequivocally politically dissident pre-1989 avant-garde art consists of a slightly different body of works that were more plaintive, subtle, and formalistically oriented, exemplified by the works of conceptual artist Xu Bing. To produce his installation *A Book from*

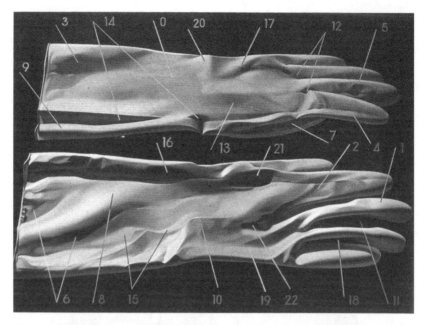

Fig. 3.2. Zhang Peili, *X Series: No. 4,* oil on canvas, 1987. Photo by the author; courtesy of the artist.

Fig. 3.3. Wu Shanzhuan, *Painted Over Rocks,* installation, 1988. Photo by the author; courtesy of the artist.

the Sky, Xu took three years to carefully fabricate thousands of fake Chinese characters that somehow "looked" like real ones, and then applied traditional Chinese bookbinding and printing techniques to produce long scrolls and traditional bonded volumes in which these faux characters were printed. His installation referred to the Buddhist idea of diligent laborer without any instrumental goals or deliberate maneuvers. However, the installation was not merely a beautifully constructed nihilist spectacle that represented a tragic vision of a futile and wasted history. The seemingly nihilist work actually contained a political message. "I felt that the Chinese language was excessively manipulated and abused during the socialist era, and I intended to purify it through this project, to restore dignify to the language by extracting the imposed messages from it and to appreciate the beauty of its form" (personal communication, December 13, 2004). Xu's art therefore offers an excellent contemporary critique on the atrocity of Maoism using a distilled combination of modernist medium and Chinese traditional symbolic repertoire.

The commonality among the wide range of pre-1989 works is that they were formalistically emulating the Western modernism while relentlessly pursuing overarching historical grand narratives. This is partly due to the fact that grand narrative, along with the black-and-white way of looking at things as preached through socialist propaganda, were deeply internalized by the 1980s avant-garde, who had lived most of their lives under Mao's regime (interviews with artist Zhang Hongtu in December 2004 and March 2005; also see Gao 1991b, 1993, 1998). It was also because through an elevated and theatrical narrative of struggle and triumph, right and wrong, good and evil, the artists' need to convey their traumatic memory under the authoritarian regime and their imperative to withdraw, to mourn, to purify and restore their previously violated self or individuality could be accommodated.

Further evidence of the affinity between grand narratives and pre-1989 avant-garde art was that the Chinese avant-garde artists of the pre-1989 era regarded the West as a divine symbolic resource. The idealization and consecration of the West in art can be observed in the avant-garde artists' avid emulation of the Western modernist style that to them symbolized everything good about Western democracy that was lacking in China. Most important, the pre-1989 avant-garde did believe that art could change society and that the idea of the West (or the Western way of life), which was still bathed in a glorified, utopian light in the Chinese public imagination, could eventually save China (Gao and Andrews 1995; interviews with various artists in 2004 and 2005).

THE DEMYSTIFICATION OF THE WEST AND THE "POSTMODERN" TRANSITION IN POST-1989 AVANT-GARDE ART

After 1989, one can identify a salient postmodern shift in the style of Chinese avant-garde art. The modernist style that was once consecrated and actively pursued by Chinese artists as both aesthetic and spiritual resource became a more individualistic, detached (from larger ideological commitment), cynical, sardonic, sensational, postmodern style. From Liu Jianhua's hypersexualized, truncated porcelain female body adorned in the traditional Chinese dress Cheongsam (figure 3.4), Wang Qingsong's photographic construction of a tongue-in-cheek, seemingly mindless co-ed hot bath and his equally whimsical contemporary re-creation of an ancient Chinese brothel, and Hu Jiemin's digitally mastered print *Raft of Medusa* depicting a group of hedonistic Chinese youth partying and drinking away on an oversized raft made of Coca-Cola and Pepsi bottles, it has become evident that the previous subversive, dissident political message in the pre-1989 Chinese avant-garde art has started to dissolve. On the other hand, the signifiers that symbolize an ever-potent and menacing global market—Coke cans, privatized bath houses that double function as brothels, skimpily covered female bodies that are frequently seen in today's Chinese media, Ronald McDonald, with all its symbolic connotations of economic and cultural imperialism—material decadence, environmental hazard, and sexual promiscuity have taken center stage and increasingly have become the target of artists' resentment and sarcasm. Chinese avant-garde art has grown out of its pre-1989 naive idealization of the West and has become more sophisticated and reflexive about both the West and its own self-identity.

Yang Fudong's video titled *Seven Chinese Intellectuals in a Bamboo Forest* is a postmodern renarration of a famous archaeological finding, a relief discovered in a Jing Dynasty tomb excavated near Nanjing that shared the same title. The seven reclusive Chinese sages in the relief are depicted as retreating and entertaining themselves with various cultural activities in a remote bamboo forest. The image of the seven reclusive sages was widely accepted as a snapshot of the intellectual par excellence of disinterested Confucian scholarship.[9] However, in Yang Fudong's postmodern rerendering of the story, the intellectuals are presented as spoiled, hedonistic urban youth who grew up with the Internet and video games, excessive media brainwash, and exceedingly felt boredom. Each anarchist "intellectual" is clothed in readily identifiable, imported European luxury brands such as Louis Vuitton and Burberry, equipped with the most updated electronic gadgets. They appeared more interested in performing the learned "coolness"

Fig. 3.4. Liu Jianhua, *Play,* color ceramic series, 2003.
Photo by the author; courtesy of the artist.

from media heroes rather than in engaging in any serious intellectual
pursuit. The whole video is a controlled ridicule of the technologiz-
ing of the Chinese self and the Westernization of the Chinese mind
and body. By resurrecting a lost civilization, Yang makes a seemingly
disinterested mockery over both the history of art and contemporary
Chinese culture.

Another similar series is Hong Hao's photographic series of
his self, "Mr. Hong," and his alternative self, "Mr. Gnoh" (Hong
deliberately reversed the order of the letters in his surname Hong
and came up with the pseudo-Western name Gnoh; figures 3.5 and
3.6). In these pictures, Hong deliberately photographed himself in
luxurious environments resembling the interiors of upscale Western
hotels or resorts in the Chinese imagination, sipping coffee or read-

Fig. 3.5. Hong Hao, *Mr. Gnoh,*
chromogenic print, 1998. Photo by
the author; courtesy of the artist.

ing business reports while listening to piano music in the lobby. Mr.
Gnoh, Hong's alternative self, has a pair of green eyes and artificially
dyed blond hair. These photos offer sardonic commentary over the
widespread Chinese admiration of Western lifestyles and how the
constructed images of Western affluence presented by the media
successfully constructed a new utopia to replace the old socialist one
in contemporary China.

The integration of the Chinese art world with the international
art market is keenly felt by Chinese artists. They become very sensitive
about what can sell and what appeals to the Western art market, and
some of them are willing to compromise or adjust for that market.
According to critic Zhu Qi and many others, Western Chinese art
collectors/dealers look for "easily identifiable" (essentialist), political-
cultural symbols/codes that are idiosyncratically Chinese (Zhu 2001).
Zhu Qui comments on the "Westernized recipe to cook the Chinese
dish" widely known and shared by successful Chinese avant-garde
artists. "Entirely political or entirely socialist works are not what
Westerners generally prefer. Westerner's taste for Chinese avant-garde
art can be categorized as follows: generally they prefer works that appear political, fashionable, sexy, subversive, and psychopathic, mixed

Fig. 3.6. Hong Hao, *Mr. Hong Please come in,* chromogenic print, 1998.
Photo by the author; courtesy of the artist.

with a little Chinese traditional element, and sprinkled with a pinch
of post-modernism" (75).

Because of the asymmetrical power present in the Chinese art
world, where the vast majority of collectors of Chinese contemporary
art are in the West, a niche for artworks that are identifiably Chinese
was created. These self-exoticizing practices were widely adopted by
Chinese artists in the 1990s (Gao Brothers 2002).

Hong Lei's painting *After Song Dynasty Zhao Ji "Loquat and
Bird"* (figure 3.7) is a poignant attack on the ill practices in today's
Chinese art world that he personally observed. He produced paint-
ings that use exactly the same format and technique as a traditional

Chinese "flower bird" painting. What he did differently, however, is to paint all the birds dead. The dead bodies of the birds in front of the beautiful peonies and orchids, traditional Chinese symbols of prosperity and serenity, are the visual incarnations of the artists' resentment toward the "selling out" of Chinese contemporary art to the West and the artist's personal struggles with manufactured "Chineseness" as part of his identity. The dead bird paintings are meant by the artist to be a refusal to offer what the Western audience expects from a Chinese painting. Hong does not want to provide just another predictably pleasant and quintessentially "Chinese" image; instead, he intentionally violates and destabilizes the established semiotics of the traditional composition. By adding elements of grossness and shock, he effectively ridicules the prevalent "faux-chinois" practice in the current Chinese art market.

Yan Lei's conceptual artwork *Forged Invitation Letter from an International Biennale* (in collaboration with Hong Lei; figure 3.8) is another controversial work that offers indignant criticism over the unlevel playing field between Western dealers and Chinese artists. By forging a fake invitation letter from the international art biennale as his own piece of art, Lei criticizes the lack of agency and autonomy that Chinese artists face from the arbitrary selection by Western curators and institutions.

Gaudy art or "pretty art" is another genre of post-1989 artwork that have become increasingly predominant. It is by nature a variation of pop art in China. The artists in this genre specialize in utilizing popular or vulgar images taken from the mass media to construct narratives about daily life in China with an exaggerated dose of vulgarity and gaudiness. It's an attempt to make the familiar absurd. Yu Youhan's chromatic print "Exactly What It Is That Makes the Modern Home So Appealing" is a witty reappropriation of the pop art work of the same title by British artist Richard Hamilton. Yu has replaced the muscular white bodybuilder in the original Hamilton image with Mao Tse-tung in a classic Mao suit with his trademark posture: both hands on the hips. Mao appears cheerful and hopeful standing in a room in an upscale residential area. The official party television station, CCTV (Chinese Central Television), is showing a speech given by Mao's successor, President Jiang Zemin. The room is filled with fashionable modern commodities such as a PC and an IKEA futon. The picture has a cheerful daydream quality to it that reminds one of the earlier socialist realist posters, but the cheerfulness is not authentic and not to be taken seriously. The demystification of both socialist values and the 1980s' idealized image of the West as a savior or harbinger of democracy is achieved through absurd juxtaposition

Fig. 3.7. Hong Lei, *After Song Dynasty Zhao Ji - Bird and Loquat,* chromogenic print, 2004. Photo by the author; courtesy of the artist.

of symbolic codes that each belong to different historical and political eras. Because of the incredible transition China has gone through in the past fifty years, the country now resembles a curiosity museum filled with residues from every earlier historical epoch.

The installation *Uncle McDonald Enters the Village* is also a notable work in this genre. It appropriates the classic socialist movie theme of Japanese invaders entering a Chinese village. In this installation, twenty or so commercial Ronald McDonald models were erected, smiling and marching toward a modern apartment complex filled with residential high-rises. Ronald McDonald, the symbol of American global economic expansion, is portrayed in an extremely unfavorable light. For the Chinese audience, the memory of Japanese invaders during the Nanjing Massacre is instantly evoked when they look at this work. It is the ultimate demonstration that the former

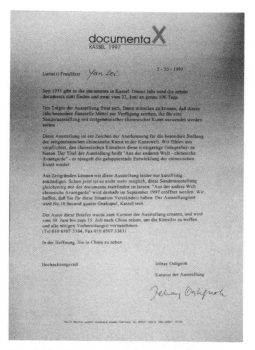

Fig. 3.8. Yan Lei, *Fake Invitation Letter,*
conceptual art, 1997. Photo by the author;
courtesy of the artist.

consecrated notion of the West in the 1980s Chinese avant-garde art
has been completely deserted.

So what exactly happened from the 1980s to the 1990s? As I
explained earlier, stylistic change can never be taken lightly as a merely
aesthetic choice or a trend. It is a sensitive indicator of each artist's
formulation of Chinese modernity. In the 1990s, the grand narrative
in Chinese avant-garde art collapsed and, along with it, an optimistic
vision of a democratic future for China. The prevalent cynicism is a
result of the contaminated image of the West in the Chinese public
sphere, as the West has been transformed from a signifier of good-
ness, honesty, rationality, and democracy in the 1980s to rampant
commercialization, dysfunctional social relationships, the decline
of community and interpersonal trust, and an unprecedented sense
of alienation in the 1990s. In the next section, we will take a closer
look at both the macro-societal transformations and the micro-level
changes in the art world.

THE MICROCOSMIC TRANSFORMATIONS IN THE CHINESE ART WORLD AROUND 1989 AND THEIR IMPLICATIONS FOR AVANT-GARDE ARTISTS

During the immediate one or two years following the Tiananmen student movement in 1989, the Chinese Communist Party (CCP) started a nationwide crackdown on its political dissidents. These dissidents were labeled as bourgeois liberalists who had chosen to succumb to the temptation of the decadent Western way of life. In the realm of education, art, and culture, the dissidents were persecuted as the polluters of "the socialist spiritual civilization." The dissident Chinese avant-garde art of the 1980s, which was on the frontier of cultural un-officialdom, was forced underground for almost three years after this new round of heightened political purging. Artists from the 1980s who exhibited Western modernist inclinations were identified as part of the cultural constituency of bourgeois liberalism, and their works were forbidden to appear in public under a new censorship law in 1990 (Gao Brothers 2002). Many artists were forced underground during the years immediately following 1989.[10]

However, since then, the overall socioeconomic structure in China has gone through a profound transformation. Market liberalization has been carried out on a larger and deeper scale, foreign capital and international nongovernmental organizations (NGOs) have arrived, social stratification has become exacerbated, and the socialist welfare system and the guarantee of life-long employment have been dismantled (Bian 1994; Khan and Riskin 2001; Tang and Parish 2000). As a result, the pursuit of personal wealth and prosperity has become the new aspiration of the nation (Davis 2000; Schein 2001). Political suppression is largely diluted and buffered by capitalist ambition and business opportunities, and the formation of a civil society is already on its way (Madsen 1998; Calhoun 1994).

The most important event of domestic structural change in the arena of modern art in response to this market takeoff was the consolidation of exhibition venues in mainland China. The Guangzhou Biennial started in 1992, and the Shanghai Biennial was established in 1996. These two events represent the most prestigious of Chinese modern art exhibitions in the 1990s—they attract thousands of works and more than one hundred artists, and both have an international draw. It is notable that both biennials happened to take place in the two most cosmopolitan Chinese cities, located at the very frontiers of market reform in China.

The Shanghai and Guangzhou biennials helped artists repair and revive the avant-garde community that was severely under attack

immediately following the Tiananmen prodemocracy student movement. Because of the dissident and transgressive quality of avant-garde
art, the consolidation of these biennials also signified the emergence
of a Chinese public sphere. Since the biennial exhibition is guaran-
teed to take place every other year, the artists are thereby assured that
their work will be presented to the public rather than to only a small
private circle of colleagues and connoisseurs. As a result, their work
incentive is protected.

The biennials have also demonstrated a considerably high degree of market efficiency. Artists, dealers, and buyers eventually have
the opportunity to meet and negotiate future transactions. Because
the final price is usually made known, artists and dealers can easily
find out which styles are "popular" at the biennials and what prices
are offered to them. In the 2002 Shanghai Biennial, because of the
number of works being shown, the exhibition took over the space of
two official galleries. Although the number of tickets sold is unknown,
witnesses reported seeing an "enormous" number of visitors that "filled
up the entire space of both of the two galleries." Becoming aware of
the huge business success of the two biennials, the curators in state-
owned museums and professors from state-sponsored national art
institutions started to provide support for avant-garde art (interview
with Huang Zhuan and Zhang Qiang, in Gao Brothers 2002). It
was clear that reinforced market intervention increased the state's
consent and tolerance toward the avant-garde previously known as
"unofficial art."

THE POST-1989 ARRIVAL OF WESTERN AGENTS AND THE RISE OF THE WEST AS THE INDISPUTABLE PRAGMATIC RESOURCE

As a result of this dynamic and complex process, the global economy
brings new actors from the West into the field of Chinese avant-garde
art and increases the exposure of that art to the international art world.
The Chinese avant-garde was introduced to the Western art market in
the late 1980s and early 1990s by successful expatriate Chinese artists
Xu Bing and Cai Guoqiang. That was only the beginning of the West's
discovery of this new body of indigenous modern art from socialist
China. During the 1990s, an unprecedented number of American and
European art agents came to China to map out the landscape of the
Chinese avant-garde. Among them were Monica Dematte, an Italian
critic and curator; Uli Sigg, the previous Swiss ambassador to China
and the owner of the largest overseas private collection of Chinese
contemporary art; Howard Farber, a former real estate investor and

an avid private art collector from New York;[11] Karen Smith, a British academic who works for a collector in the United States but also an art consultant and curator herself; Barbara London, an associate curator from the Museum of Modern Art's Department of Film and Video, who "hikes the back roads of the Middle Kingdom in her quest for the best Chinese Media Art,"[12] accompanied by F. D. P. Henryz, a painter from the Netherlands. Other noteworthy names in the long list include Robert Bernell, a publisher and the prominent owner of renowned bookstore Timezone 8 in the newly established 798 art district; Australian dealer Brian Wallace, the manager of the Red Gate Gallery in Beijing that deals in exclusively Chinese contemporary art; Scott Savitt, the creator and maintainer of the Web site BeijingScene,[13] as well as Lorenz Helbling, an art dealer who resides in Shanghai and hosts a Web site titled "Shanghai Art." Barbara London's "China Stir-Fry" Web site devotes a few lines to delineate the ambiguous identity and missions of these Western agents:

> Helbling, along with Karen Smith and Hans van Dijk in Beijing, have important but precariously defined roles in China. They deal in contemporary Chinese art, nearly exclusively to foreigners. Chinese citizens only buy traditional art and realist paintings, the art forms sanctioned by the government. China, now in an "emerging" phase of development, looks to its historic roots for self-understanding. Art that falls outside state-defined parameters only gets shown in homes or in unpublicized fringe venues.[14]

These art agents started their search in major coastal cities such as Beijing, Shanghai, and Guangzhou and afterward excursed deep into China's hinterland, Wuhan, Chendu, and Chongqing. Each one of them embodies various roles and carries multiple responsibilities. They are often simultaneously artists, dealers, curators, journalists, and academics, although some of them act exclusively as agents sent by major art institutions or private dealers from Europe, Australia, or the United States. Their arrival added a new spin of power and resource into the post-1989 Chinese avant-garde art world, bringing with them unexpected energy, excitement, ambition, as well as dismay and frustration. Before the West discovered the Chinese avant-garde, artists working in this specific group had always struggled between political persecution of the state (Kraus 1991, 1989, 2004; Andrews 1994; Andrews and Gao 1995; Andrews and Shen 1998) and a lack of enthusiasm and support from the domestic audience and private collectors. They were also alienated by antagonism and deliberate marginalization by their colleagues in the state-sanctioned artist guilds.[15] As Chinese modern art becomes more integrated into the international art market, the interest and acknowledgment shown by the Western art world provide these artists with both a long-overdue exit from their dismayed past and an exciting passport toward numerous opportunities overseas. More important, they have regained their sense of self-worth from acknowledgment and recognition by the Western art world (Gao Brothers 2002).

However, the increased involvement of Western agents in the Chinese art world has unleveled the power dynamic of the field. The artists have more or less lost their autonomy in the current structure, and new anxieties have emerged. First, increased exposure to and promotion by the West turned out to be accessible only to the very few artists who enjoy phenomenal success in the international art world. Artists in mainland China feel obliged to self-promote to Western curators or collectors, often through means of exaggeration or distortion of facts. British art historian Karen Smith first arrived in Beijing in 1992 to study contemporary Chinese art. She wanted to find out what were the most influential works from the 1989 exhibition that was forced to be shut down by the state. However, she was constantly confused by the artists she interviewed as each artist she met claimed that he or she was the creator of the influential piece from that exhibition. She said, "I felt that I could never figure out who I could trust" (Gao Brothers 2002: 35).

Second, informal networks are institutionalized by established artists to exclude newcomers. Artist and curator Zhu Qi (2001) has illustrated the common scenario of Western agents' search in China. These Western investigators arrive in Beijing with one or two phone numbers of local contacts, do their interviews, stay for a day or two to get to know the artist, and then hurry toward their next target with a new phone number of some other "must-know" artist. However, most of them do not realize that the circle of introduction is an implicitly enclosed and exclusionary one that works to prevent the out-group artists from obtaining any "international" exposure.

Third, the Internet has become a crucial venue for Chinese artists to sell their work overseas. It has become a stage where the asymmetrical power in the international art market is played out. The most prominent and influential internet Web sites, such as China-AvantGarde.Com and Chinese-Art.Com,[16] are owned and operated by dealers who are themselves Westerners. They have connections with successful artists, art critics, and curators in China and major art institutions and galleries in the West. Information (articles, archives, news) on these Web sites is updated frequently, and the coverage is usually comprehensive and professional. Their Web site design is invariably sleek and sophisticated. On these sites, established artists are introduced, and prominent art critics are featured with their personal columns. The working language is English. Both the professional and comprehensive content and the sophisticated writing indicate that their target readers are experienced Western dealers or modern art connoisseurs. The artwork presented on the Web sites are usually not priced; however, contact information is available for buyers who are interested in negotiating the price.

The less successful/less well-known artists, however, do not enjoy the luxury of "Internet management." They mostly design their own Web sites, individually or collaboratively.[17] These sites are large in number but are usually designed with less technical competency and commercial sophistication compared with the former ones. They are updated irregularly or not at all. The default working language on these Web sites is also English, which indicates that these artists are also trying to present their works to an imagined Western buyer. In terms of verbal presentation, the written English on these Web sites is usually not fluent and often carries grammatical mistakes. In terms of both their depth and their breadth, the quality of articles on these sites is usually not comparable to the aforementioned ones. These sites usually focus on rather narrow tasks, such as publicizing one artist or a small group of less renowned artists. Also, the descriptions of artists on these Web sites are curiously pompous and inflated, with many claiming that the featured artist is the "greatest" or "most important" Chinese modern artist, which disconcertingly reveals their insecurity and desperation for attention. Some works on these Web sites carry prices. It is evident that as a result of these sites' incompetent visual/verbal presentation, lack of professionalism, and a tangible eagerness to sell, these lesser-known artists are stuck in similarly inferior positions over the Internet as they are in real life.

Fourth, as I explicated earlier, because there are few domestic collectors of Chinese contemporary art, Chinese artists are obliged to play up the mythical aspects of their work utilizing easily identifiable Chinese symbols that represent the remoteness and strangeness of their own culture—in other words, accommodating to the exotic fantasy of an audience in the West who understands little about the complex semiotics behind the artworks. Artists such as Hong Lei[18] and Zhang Huan consciously use their works to criticize the "self-exoticization" practice. Hong poked fun at the highly mannered practice of self-exoticization with his dead bird series, while Zhang adopted an "occidentalist" strategy and rendered the West as "exotic" and "strange" in his self-created language. Zhang Huan's acclaimed performance series "My America," "My New York," and "My Australia" were complex yet high-intensity symbolic capsules that hint at the foreignness, absurdity, and occasional barbarian quality of existence in developed contemporary Western societies. In his performance "My America," Zhang constructed a spectacle in the Seattle Asian Art Museum. He set up the space in a way to make it resemble a large prison. Then he sat in lotus position at the center of the space while fifty or so naked Americans circled around him in classical Tibetan pilgrimage ritual. In the next sequence, the Americans scream and jump like primates while throwing pieces of bread at the artist.

Since the end of the 1990s, there has been a rising discourse of authenticity among critics of Chinese contemporary art (Wu 2000; Zhu 2001; Nuridsany 2004; Pollack 2004; Vine 2004). Some art historians who study Chinese avant-garde art advocate to cease calling today's Chinese contemporary artists "avant-garde," as the original meaning of the term no longer sustains in reality and has possibly already been abused (Wu 2000; Bernell 2002; Wu and Philips 2004). For many critics, the Chinese avant-garde in the 1980s experienced a loss of innocence. This chapter has come to show that the stylistic change from learned modernism in the 1980s Chinese avant-garde art to the 1990 postmodern art has indisputable sociological basis. The conditions that facilitated the shift are at once tangible structural changes that take place in the front stage and underlying mechanisms such as the gradual undermining of symbolic legitimacy of the West as a sacred signifier for Chinese modernity.

CONCLUSION: THE MEANING OF STYLE AND THE CULTURAL-PRAGMATIC DISSONANCE IN POST-1989 CHINESE AVANT-GARDE ART

I would like to propose a "symbolic-pragmatic dissonance" paradigm to account for the "postmodern" shift observed in the post-1989 era. As I have shown, stylistic decisions in Chinese modern or contemporary art have always carried surplus symbolic meanings with deep social, historical referents; they have rarely been truly autonomous or self-referential as most art historians believe them to be. To create or adopt the "right" style (i.e., traditional or modern [Western], realist or abstract, figurative or nonfigurative) was the key for Chinese artists who have lived at the periphery of the global economy and global culture to establish their identity, as well as to express their individual vision of Chinese modernity.

Style is the most sensitive indicator of aesthetic, cultural, and political preference for these artists. It also determines the intellectual and political camp with which they represent or feel affiliation. Early Chinese modernists in the 1920s and 1930s used a blend of realist and nonfigurative techniques to search for a middle ground between Western figurative oil painting and traditional Chinese literati painting, but the symbolic imperative behind that effort was to build a modern China with both Western technology and a rich Chinese cultural heritage. The official style of the socialist era was socialist realism because the Western modernist style was perceived to symbolize the moral decadence and mental bankruptcy of the capitalist West, which was the enemy and the axis of evil for all socialist nations during the Cold War. Socialist realism was avidly emulated by Chinese official artists because the very "Westernness" in this style signifies "modern," and its natural affinity with the Soviet Union gave it political legitimacy in China during the Cultural Revolution years.

Pre-1989 avant-garde artists stood in opposition to the official ideology. Because memory of the traumatic Cultural Revolution still persisted in the 1980s, the official socialist realist style of the time was perceived as a contaminated and obsolete signifier for the type of modernity that these artists envisioned. The pre-1989 avant-garde embraced humanism, freedom, individual rights, and dignity, and it saw the democratic West as a source of symbolic inspiration. Because market liberalization did not really take off on any large scale in China before the 1990s, the West existed in pre-1989 avant-garde art largely as a spiritual Mecca, a purifying source, a symbolic utopia.

This sacred/profane dichotomy that put socialism and Western democracy on the oppositional pole of Chinese modernization prospects (rational, democratic, humanistic Western democracy vs. irrational, undemocratic, inhuman Chinese socialism) inevitably consecrated the West in the post–Cultural Revolution, pre-1989 Chinese intellectual sphere. This shift was made evident through the pursuit of the Western modernist style in pre-1989 avant-garde art. Ironically, the pre-1989 avant-garde continued the socialist state's usage of grand narratives to counteract it with their own version of utopia. The pre-1989 avant-garde emphasized both the purity and the rationalization of the form as well as poignant criticisms of state violence. Their works carried a sensationalized sense of theatrical tragedy.

In the post-1989 avant-garde art world, accompanied by China's accelerated economic liberalization and international integration, the West has more or less lost its symbolic legitimacy, as its meaning has increasingly become associated with the negative consequences of marketization. In the post-1989 Chinese consciousness, the West and the market have become increasingly synonymous. As a result, the West has picked up a broad range of undesirable symbolic connotations, such as greediness, sexual promiscuity, excessive materialism, techno-centrism, social alienation, and the inhumanness of capitalist labor. Chinese avant-garde artists have been very sensitive in observing this post-1989 shift of symbolic paradigm in contemporary Chinese culture. Confronting unprecedented commercialization and advertisement in everyday life, when previously valuable feelings or objects in life and in the art world seemed to be immediately exchangeable on the market, the pre-1989 metanarrative inevitably broke down.

The demystification of the West in Chinese art is also accompanied by a loss of innocence on the part of Chinese artists. Contradictory to the loss of symbolic legitimacy of the West, the West as an institution has increasingly gained power in the Chinese art world. The arrival of Western agents changed the power dynamics in the Chinese art world. Artists increasingly find themselves in a position of struggling entrepreneurs, negotiating in a market operated under an asymmetrical power structure, where most of their buyers are from abroad. A certain niche for contemporary Chinese artworks that are identifiably "Chinese" or "postsocialist" has already been created.

I therefore argue that artists' acute awareness of the declining stature of the West in the symbolic realm is in radical contrast to the ascending power it enjoys in the pragmatic realm of the art world. The dissonance and dissension between the two compelled artists to create tremendously poignant and powerful works in the post-Tiananmen era that are postmodern in nature. Postmodern art, along with its trademark sarcasm, irony, cynicism, mindless simulacrum and pastiche, tough-in-cheek flamboyance, pleasure principle, and guilt-free expressions of violence, was the best stylistic signifier chosen by the artists to convey their sense of disorientation, frustration, and exhausted excitement in the post-1989 world.

EPILOGUE: TOWARD A MEANINGFUL SOCIOLOGY OF THE AVANT-GARDE

The discussions over the nature and production of avant-garde art have always been a part of the core literature of the sociology of art and culture. Renato Poggioli (1968) and Peter Burger (1984) both understand avant-garde art to be a joint effort of sociopolitical endeavors (socially progressive, antibourgeois in nature) and radical artistic intentions, which include sheer innovation of style and technique, formalistic purity, and a resolute breach from both the establishment and the commercial leanings of the mainstream culture. Frankfurt School thinkers Theodor Adorno (1984, 1993) and Walter Benjamin

(1968a, 1968b, 1978) hailed the art avant-garde as the final champion for the freedom of human subjectivity during the high capitalist era in the face of the deadening cultural homogeneity created by a predatory cultural industry. Clement Greenberg (1939) insists that avant-garde art is the only form of art that has a historical mission of change and progress, and thereby it is the only means through which culture can survive and keep moving forward.

Despite the philosophers' and cultural critics' ardent enthusiasm toward the modernist avant-garde, sociologists exemplified by Pierre Bourdieu find the romanticized notion of an emancipating and icono-clastic avant-garde art (or the "autonomous art," as Bourdieu terms it) deeply problematic. In *The Field of Cultural Production* (1993) and *Rules of Art* (1996), Bourdieu criticizes the formalist, neo-Kantian ideal of "art for art's sake" to be empirically false and politically reaction-ary. Bourdieu frames his own analysis in a paradigm of "habitus" and "field." He argues that the system of aesthetics and taste are socially situated and historically constructed.[19] The institutionalization of the field of autonomous art, he maintains, is a result of structural domination and subjective struggles carried out by reflexive actors (artists, writers, composers) within various intellectual and artistic fields of cultural production. Bourdieu emphasizes that to accept the formalist claim is to turn a blind eye to the concrete historical process of the "consecration" of art (he also calls it the legitimization of a "pure gaze"). He debunks the very notion of "autonomous art" by pointing out the socioeconomic location of the cultural producers and their individual or collective habitus as a result of it. The struggles between cultural producers in the field forces the actors to reproduce or further mystify the notion of "autonomous art" and subsequently reinforce the established order of social distinction.[19]

American sociologist Diana Crane (1987) has offered a more value-neutral yet no less structuralist account of the avant-garde in her study of the New York art world from the 1940s to the 1980s. Her 1987 book is still a watermark in the studies of the Western avant-garde due to the unrivaled thoroughness of her historical research. However, it lacks a crucial sensitivity toward the symbolic dimension of the cul-tural change of the time.[20] Under Crane's and many other American cultural production researchers' theorems of art, culture, and society, cultural products are mostly the outcomes of changes in pragmatic, instrumental factors such as institutional support for museums, the expansion of private galleries, imperatives for a larger-scale public education, and gentrification of impoverished communities.

In my opinion, the biggest mistake of the cultural production approach is that it flattens or disregards the meaning of the style of the artwork so that either all styles become interchangeable or a style is only significant because of its pronounced ability to offend or attract the public. If all that is important about art is the creation of more paintings to fill up newly created museums' walls or to be taught in colleges and public high schools funded by the postwar National Endowment for the Arts, exactly why did it have to be the abstract expressionism in the 1940s and pop art in the 1960s?

I believe one cannot disregard the protagonists of the artistic movement (i.e., the artists) by assuming that artworks and art styles are merely results of social construction or capitalistic manipulation (DeNora 1995; Peterson 1997). A social scientist needs to unpack the complex symbolic reservoir behind an artwork and its chronological context to understand the meaning system that sustains and inspires the creation of avant-garde art. Crane's study, along with many other works by the sociologists who share the production of culture perspective, are more or less marked by the same unwillingness to address the autonomy of culture. In other words, the production of culture perspective tends to treat art as a commodity in the capitalist society, not as fundamentally different from any other. Thus, this view fails to see artists as reflexive and culturally informed actors, and their art works as meaning-laden statements reflecting their specific vision of life and ideological/artistic commitment.

Bourdieu and the production of culture scholars' overly reductionist and instrumental understanding of art and culture have become increasingly criticized in the fields of sociology and cultural studies in recent years (Calhoun et al. 1993; Alexander 1995). Sociologists of art and culture today (Eyerman and Magnus 1998; Eyerman 2005) have been making great efforts to steer away from the previous models that dealt exclusively with the institutional and economic aspects of art production. They have opened up new grounds for interpreting the expressive quality and cultural meaning of avant-garde art in an increasingly disenchanted and segmented contemporary society. This chapter finds itself among this new line of cultural sociological thinking about art and culture.

NOTES

1. Avant-garde art in the West has always been associated with art modernism, which started with French impressionist paintings in the late nineteenth century and ended approximately in the 1960s with abstract expressionism (even though some critics argue that it has found its continuation in postmodernist art as the third-wave modernism). Transplanting the term *avant-garde* from Western art history to the analysis of Chinese contemporary

art has been widely questioned and contested by art historian and critics who study Chinese modernist art. See Wu Hung (2000)'s "Canceled: Exhibiting Experimental Art in China." For discussion of the meaning of this term in Western culture and social theory, see the last section of this chapter.

2. I have specific reasons for insisting on providing my own formulation of a sociohistorical framework within which the 1980s and 1990s avant-garde art will be situated as an organic and continuous development of Chinese modernism that started in the early twentieth century. Although many have discussed modernity in Chinese art (e.g., Fong 2001; Hay 2001), I believe a framework of "Chinese art modernism" needs to be established to appropriately examine Chinese avant-garde art in its proper historical context. However, my questions concerning Chinese art modernism differ greatly from that of literature studies or art history. Although I reject the structural determinism of the production of culture perspective, unlike an art historian or a literary critic, I see a formulation of Chinese modernism to be sociologically significant and helpful for the following reasons:

   a. The emergence and development of Chinese modernism coincides with China's various modernization projects in the context of an asymmetrical global power structure. For example, the first-wave Chinese art modernism was part of a larger reaction against traditional, outdated feudal norms and conventions, and the second wave was a disillusioned protest against failed socialism (in that case, the Cultural Revolution). The postmodernism (what I see as the fourth-wave Chinese modernism) of the 1990s is a response to the increased exposure artists obtained from the internationalization of the Chinese contemporary art world of this era. It cannot be understood if we pay attention only to the very unpostmodern, subsistence-level existence of the vast majority of Chinese citizens in mainland China today.
   b. The internal logic of the Chinese modernist style is fundamentally different from that of Western modernism because it is developed from its own very specific historical context. Namely, unlike Western art modernism, which arose as a critical, autonomous reaction against both artistic convention and the commercialized culture under high capitalism, capitalism had long been absent in the Chinese modernist tradition. Instead of ceaseless pursuit of sheer originality and formalistic purity, the negotiation between the Chinese and Western stylistic elements remains central and is highly sensitized. In other words, the Chinese modern artists cared less about originality per se but used their artistic style as a medium through which to have a meaningful dialogue over modernity with their intended audience.
   c. Since, by definition, the establishment of the very identity of "Chinese modernism" is feasible only with Western modernism as its reference, we are facing a tradition of learned and contrived "modernism" in modern and contemporary Chinese art, with latent

and constantly shifting discourse of the West as a symbolic axis that generates meaning. Thus, the question of authenticity in Chinese avant-garde art remains inescapable.

3. *Chinese modernism in art* is a term that I'm interested in developing because of its theoretical significance and the advantage of using this term to facilitate comparative research in modern/contemporary artistic and cultural development across national boundaries.

4. It is notable that the earliest cohort of Chinese modernist artists and intellectuals almost invariably emerged from members of the expatriate Chinese community who managed to travel outside China and studied in the West. It is a resonance of the European modernists who were born in the cultural periphery of Europe. Most of them also strived to study and work in a central cultural locale and subsequently made a name for themselves. (Berlin was the destination for Strindberg and Ibsen, as Paris was for Chagall and Malevich.)

5. The high Mao era included "the Great Leap Forward" (1958–1963), a well-known CCP-led industrialization frenzy, and the Cultural Revolution (1966–1976). I acknowledge that socialist realism (not social realism) has more affinity with academic painting than the Western modernist tradition, but, as I argue in the epilogue, Chinese modernism has its own logic of development that does not follow strict formalistic or aesthetic principles but sociological and symbolic ones.

6. The neotraditionalist style was technically very similar to traditional Chinese ink brush painting, with renewed themes of praising the beautiful land and the great working people of socialist China.

7. A good example of socialist realism in literature is Zhou Libo's large-volume socialist trilogy, a novel titled *Bao Feng Zhou Yu* (The Wild Wind and Sudden Rain 暴风骤雨.).

8. Chinese society in the late 1970s and early 1980s was caught between two worlds. It had not left the afflicting memories of the Cultural Revolution behind, while a heightened state of economic liberalization that we would later observe in the 1990s had not yet flourished. Young people of the time had just obtained permission to pursue their education in colleges, in which they indulged themselves in absorbing any piece of information about the West, regardless whether it was on art, literature, music, philosophy, or technology. The common sentiment of the time was that the brief freedom granted to individuals might soon be taken away by another political turmoil without giving any warning.

9. Confucianism preaches active engagement in government and social affairs. The disinterested recluses in *Seven Chinese Intellectual* were idealized only for the reason that they have previously served in the court where their progressive views were not accepted, so subsequently all of them demanded a voluntary early retirement to preserve their personal integrity.

10. Immediately after 1989, avant-garde groups continued to congregate and held small-scale exhibitions at private homes (Gao Brothers 2002). Chinese avant-garde art thus struggled to be public for four to five

years, and many artists and critics were tormented by an overarching sense of despair and hopelessness (Gao Brothers 2002). During this time, a lot of artists managed to flee China to seek alternative venues to present their work.

11. See www.forbes.com/investmentnewsletters/2005/02/02/cz_ms_ 0202soapbox_inl.html, retrieved March 23, 2005.

12. Quote from London's personal Web site "China StirFry."

13. See www.scene.co.cn/so_menu.html, retrieved May 3, 2003.

14. Seehttp://adaweb.walkerart.org/context/stir-fry/index1.html, retrieved May 3, 2003.

15. Seewww.guxiang.com/yishu/others/shalong/200103/200103190046. htm for traditional artists' unfavorable and antagonistic comments toward Chinese avant-garde artists.

16. Chinese-Art.com, a major online portal for Chinese contemporary art, has been shut down since 2004.

17. For example, http://go.6to23.com/muktiye/ and www.sunday-art. com/service.htm.

18. I have talked extensively about Hong Lei's dead bird series in the previous section on post-1989 Chinese contemporary art.

19. Bourdieu states that the logic within the field of "autonomous" art is the logic of "the economic world reversed." It requires artists to delay recognition by the masses or any form of popular acclaim by earning a reputation within the field first. As a result, the seemingly disinterested, "formalistically correct" cultural product can be picked out by the taste makers or gatekeepers in the field (e.g., gallery owners, critics, etc.) and be sold as a distinctive form of cultural product to an exclusively small circle of collectors, who are exempted from the brutish need of economic necessity, and who possess the right amount of capital (both cultural and economic) to appreciate and acquire it. The political implication of this process, according to Bourdieu, is that the economic inequality and social hierarchy that are usually laid out in crude material form is hereby legitimatized and naturalized culturally in the name of formalism and the autonomy of art.

20. Crane's contention that "the growth of the plastic arts was part of a larger phenomenon which included the expansion of artistic activities ..., that flourished as a result of greatly increased allocations of resources from other social institutions, presumably reflecting a redefinition of the importance or relevance of these arts in American society," was limited and somewhat reductionist in vision.

CHAPTER 4

Seeker of the Sacred

A Late Durkheimian
Theory of the Artist

Steve Sherwood

I wish to draw on Émile Durkheim's late masterwork, *The Elementary Forms of the Religious Life,* in offering a new theory of the artist. There has been little recent innovation within the realm of the sociology of art. Indeed, it remains, along with the sociology of religion, one of the "backwaters" of discipline. This is not due to a lack of empirical discovery but rather to a lack of any significant theorizing about the artist and their art. What Clifford Geertz said nearly forty years ago about anthropology is still true of the sociology of art today: there is a wealth of empirical studies, but almost no theoretical innovation. The advance of knowledge within an academic discipline is driven not merely by a collection of "facts" but by the development of theoretical models that ultimately enable those "facts" to speak. New ideas in the sociology of art require new theoretical applications. And all theoretical innovation relies on constant reference to, and reinterpretation of, the classical foundations of those theories. In returning to Durkheim's (2001) *Elementary Forms of the Religious Life* (hereafter "EFRL"), then, we look to advance the understanding of the artist by deepening our engagement with a frequently misunderstood and underutilized resource. In theoretical terms, classical models enable contemporary advances. As Jeffrey Alexander (1989) once put it, "While arguing about Durkheim, we are really arguing about contemporary ideas, indeed about contemporary society" (147). This view, of course, echoes Durkheim's statement on the very first page of the EFRL that the primary goal of sociology is "first and foremost to explain a current reality, something close to us and consequently capable of affecting our ideas and actions" (3). The artist, I believe, has such relevance and it will be my aim in this chapter to suggest some new directions in assessing that significance.

At the core of the argument in the EFRL is what Alexander (1989) refers to as the "spiritual program of Durkheim's later writings" (143). It is this "late" model of Durkheim's theorizing, as rendered in Alexander's appropriation for purposes of establishing a "cultural sociology," with which I will work here (for more recent applications by Alexander et al. of the late Durkheimian model, see Alexander and Smith 2005). Alexander (1989) asserts that Durkheim made a shift in his late theory, a "symbolic breakthrough," to a "religious model of social order" (144). Social institutions, in this later view of Durkheim's, "were composed of crystallized emotions, not material forms," and this required a "new understanding of the role that ritual, sacred authority and representation played in secular life." Alexander sees the importance of Durkheim's "breakthrough" as offering an important corrective to the structural determinism and reductionism of much of sociological analysis: "Durkheim's subjective structuralism has represented for sociological thought the theoretical antithesis to the objective structuralism of Marx" (1989:146).

In understanding the "religious force" that permeated society and its institutions ("Everything is religious in principle," Alexander quotes him as saying), Durkheim was demanding that the import and power of the sacred be acknowledged and recognized.

Drawing on this "late" Durkheimian approach, then, we can, first and foremost, assert the *reality* of the sacred and sacrality within society (Sherwood 1998:47–56).

For our purposes, Durkheim is useful in understanding the artist in new and important ways. In terms of public representation, collective forces are generally seen to repress and inhibit the artist (e.g., repression and conformity) and the "individual" is seen to be the primary producer behind artistic production (the so-called art hero). Durkheim offers a corrective to this popular view and enables us to consider the structural dimensions of subjectivity in considering art and artist, what Alexander refers to as the strong relationship between "structure and meaning" (i.e., freedom and the meaning that it provides is only possible *through* the structures of society and not merely in spite of them).

Durkheim argued that ritual conduct related to the ways in which *mana* or force was managed within both primitive and modern society. Durkheim's analysis of the relationship between the totem and the Australian aboriginals for whom it was so meaningful, for example, enables us to consider the significance of the image to the artist. Every artist works, somehow, within the realm of images. And the power of contemporary images can certainly be related to the "totemic principle" or force of which Durkheim speaks.

One of the important benefits of Alexander's reappraisal of the late Durkheim has been to supplement Durkheim's original "religious" conception at the level of theory with more recent methodologies capable of evoking this less visible dimension. In the past two decades, Alexander and his followers have drawn on hermeneutical, phenomenological, and narrative strategies to interpret the collective representations out of which the collective consciousness emerges (Alexander, Smith, and Sherwood 1993:10–14). Where public opinion often perceives artists to be excessively independent, the sociology of art generally errs in the opposite direction: sociologists of art generally neglect the creative process by which the artist is defined. The "spiritual" paradigm of Durkheim, then, as well as the Alexanderian appropriation of this paradigm through more recent interpretive approaches, enables us to begin to explore the artist in more detail than offered by more conventional sociologies.

In undertaking such explorations, I am not suggesting that this sacred dimension of the subjective orientation of the artist is the *only* element in either the creative process or the public representation of the artist. There have been many useful studies within neo-Marxist, neo-Weberian, interactionist, and postmodern paradigms that consider the structural challenges to the artist: artists are at the mercy of their "habitus" (Pierre Bourdieu's early study that alludes to the "social aging" of the artist, among other things), that the so-called artist industry commodifies both artists and their work (Griselda Pollock), that artists are more the result of a set of contingent and instrumental factors than any "romantic" creative intentionality (George Kubler), and that artists rely on a web of supportive interactions, a kind of "art world," to provide their creative context (Howard Becker) (Bourdieu 1988:75–103; Pollock 1980:57–96; Kubler 1962; Becker 1982).

All of these studies have clearly been important in understanding the actions and products of the artist. My argument is that while they are necessary, they are not sufficient. If the realm of the sacred is a reality for society, as Durkheim tells us it is, then it is certainly a reality for the artist as well.

THE ELEMENTARY FORMS OF THE CREATIVE LIFE: THE ARTIST AS A SEEKER OF THE SACRED

To consider the artist as a "religious" actor, in Durkheim's sense, we must see that the "cult of the artist" involves all of the same ritual categories that Durkheim (2001) asserted to be at the heart of religious belief: "the distinction between sacred and profane things, the notions of soul, of spirit, of mythical personalities, of a national and even international divinity, the negative cult and its extreme form of ascetic practices, rites of oblation and communion, imitative rites, commemorative rites, piacular rites—nothing essential is missing" (310). All of these practices comprise what might be seen as a kind of devotedness or devotion and, indeed, the origin of the word *sacred* comes from the Latin word *sacrare*, "to devote."

At the heart of Durkheim's EFRL is his assertion that the universe is fundamentally divided into two, primordial sets of categories, the sacred and the profane. He asserts that all religious belief is founded on this distinction. The sacred is that which must be protected from the profane and which the profane may not touch. Whole series of rituals and beliefs are organized around constituting the realm of the sacred and keeping it "pure."

What was most sacred to the aboriginal cultures of Australia about which Durkheim wrote was the totem, the characteristic symbol or emblem by which they identified their tribe or clan and that they placed at the center of their ritual ceremonies and tribal rites. "The totem is above all a symbol, a material expression of something else," Durkheim writes, "but of what?" (154). For Durkheim, the totem is symbolic of the creative force of society itself. He asserts that the totem becomes invested with social force through the feelings that tribal members have for it and what it represents to them. This collective feeling is what Durkheim refers to as the "totemic principle" and represents *mana*, or the spiritual force that underlies society. It is the emotional "glue" of society, if you will. And it is this force that endows merely ordinary or mundane things with the force or power of the sacred: "There are occasions when this strengthening and vivifying action of society is especially apparent," Durkheim writes. "Within a crowd moved by common passion, we become susceptible to feelings and action of which we are incapable on our own. And when the crowd is dissolved, when we find ourselves alone again and fall back to our usual level, we can then measure how far we were raised above ourselves" (157).

Although it has been given little attention, a central foundation of Durkheim's argument is the idea that these religious forces are also *imaginative* forces. The "heightening" effect of the sacred, the "elevation" of the social actor, is the result of both the physical and the mental power of the totemic principle. The totem represents both a kind of power and a kind of ideal. That is, Durkheim is arguing for the creative potential within society being situated within the ability of "the ideal" to "transfigure" empirical reality in such a way as to endow it with the force and power of the sacred, which, Durkheim states, is synonymous with the ideal: "the sacred character that garbs a thing is not implicated in its intrinsic features, it is added to them" (173–75).

So Durkheim's theory of the sacred is also a theory of the imagination. Witness the power of the sacred and the imaginative transformation it provides, as Durkheim relates it:

> From the physical point of view, a man is just a system of cells, from the mental point of view just a system of representations; from either perspective, he differs from the animals only in degrees. Yet society conceives him, and obliges us to conceive him, as invested with a character sui generis that isolates him, holds at a distance all rash encroachments and, in a word, imposes respect. This dignity which puts him into a class by himself appears to us as one of his distinctive attributes, although we can find nothing in the empirical nature of man which justifies it. A cancelled postage stamp may be worth a fortune; but surely this value is in no way implied in its natural properties. In a sense our representation of the external world is undoubtedly a mere fabric of hallucinations, for the odors, tastes, and colors that we put into bodies are not really there, or at least, they are not such as we perceive them. (172)

This "hallucinogenic" character stems from the power of the sacred, and the power of the sacred is both absolute and, in some sense, unreal or imagined. For Durkheim's purposes, not only may we apply his "spiritual" model of society to the realm of art and artist, but we must do so. For his argument relies on the idea that *all* institutions within society are modeled upon this framework, constituting what Edward Shils once referred to as a kind of "center and periphery" relationship (Shils 1975). So if Durkheim can so strongly assert (as he does repeatedly, from the beginning to the end of the EFRL) that science derives from religion (where else could it possibly come from?, he asks), certainly there can be no doubt that art does, too. And if that is the case, if all institutions grew out of an undifferentiated religious complex, then the artist must be understood as having a "religious" dimension in the same sense. The separation between the ideal and the real, then, requires a kind of "faith," and it is precisely this confidence that the religious imagination can provide. But if imagination is a form of religion, religion is no less a form of imagination (i.e., an imaginative accomplishment). The sacred as a form of the ideal, Durkheim states in many ways, is *imagined* first: "religion is above all a system of notions by which individuals *imagine* the society to which they belong and their obscure yet intimate relations with that society. This is its primordial role; and although this representation is metaphorical and symbolic, it is not inaccurate" (171, emphasis mine).

As we have seen, the totem may be seen to embody or represent the creative principle or creative force. In the closing paragraphs of the EFRL, Durkheim tells us that "society wields a creative power that no palpable being can equal," and, earlier, that "society is constantly creating new sacred things" (342, 160). To understand the artist within this framework, we must see the artist as both working with and constantly in pursuit of such creative energy or force. The historical development of art and the artist in the West has involved not only both a "cult of art" as well as a "cult of the artist," but also the "cult of the image." For our purposes, we can define creative production as the process of realizing or articulating or bringing images to life, usually through the process of synthesizing old, new, and often disassociated images. In this sense, the artwork can itself be seen as a kind of totemic emblem, the artist and the public may be seen as the worshippers who revere and worship it, and the relationship on which this "worship" is based may be regarded as a "religious" one.

It is in this way that we may define the artist (and, indeed, the public), in a creative sense, as a seeker of the sacred. And by so doing, we may also draw on yet another central element from Durkheim's masterwork: the idea of the soul. A "spiritual" perspective on society and the very idea of the sacred presupposes the idea of a component of the social actor that responds to such a dimension. What is the soul? According to Durkheim in chapter 8 of the EFRL entitled "The Notion of the Soul," it is "a particular application of beliefs" relating to the sacred" (192–93). Indeed, it represents the most sacred part of us, as opposed to the body, which is profane. More important, however, Durkheim says that the soul "represents in us something other than ourselves," specifically that it conveys the idea that "there is something divine in us." The idea of the soul has received only scant attention in the literature on Durkheim as well as in other academic disciplines, but the rare work that has been done relying on the concept is notable both for its interdisciplinarity as well as its quality (Sherwood 1998; Fields 1996:193–203; Katz 1996:545–82).

Elsewhere, I have argued that Durkheim's definition of the soul, as with his definitions of the sacred and society itself, involves a certain conceptual tension (Sherwood 1998). When Durkheim writes of the soul that it is the core of our "moral conscience" and that "it seems to be a higher external power handing down the law and judging us, but also helping and sustaining us," he is actually defining the soul as a manifestation of the totemic principle, in two different (sometimes complementary, sometimes conflicting) ways: the soul as a kind of energy or force that "helps and sustains us," yet also as "higher external power" that "judges" us (208). The first is what I have called the "immanent" model of the soul—that is, the idea of the soul as primarily a kind of energy or force—whereas the second is what I refer to as the "transcendent" model of the soul, which emphasizes the idea of the soul as being a kind of ideal or representation.

For his conception of the soul (and the sacred) as a kind of immanent force or power, Durkheim offers the example of the corroboree, the ritual gathering of tribal members in celebration of significant occasions, in which "their proximity generates a kind of electricity that quickly transports them to an extraordinary degree of exaltation" (161–62). The second, more transcendent model is pointed to by Durkheim when he asserts that the ideals or representations at the heart of the French Revolution—"homeland, liberty and reason"—symbolized a "cult of Reason" that transformed "purely secular" into "sacred" things, an example of how "society consecrates … things, especially ideas."

I will consider each of these models in turn: the "immanent" model in regard to the creative process of the artist, the second in regard to the artist as a collective representation. The first will rely on a largely phenomenological approach, the second on a more hermeneutic orientation.

THE IMMANENT MODEL OF THE SOUL: THE ARTIST AND THE CREATIVE PROCESS

The "soul" of the artist is constituted by the same kind of creative power or force that animates society itself, which Durkheim believes to be the most creative entity there is. This pervasive, animating, electricity-like force acts on us in *spiritual* ways, according to Durkheim: "Since it is in spiritual ways that social pressure exercises itself, it could not fail to give men the idea that outside themselves there exist one or several powers, both moral and, at the same time, efficacious, upon which they depend" (239). Thus, he says, "we must conclude that the soul, in a general way, is none other than the totemic principle incarnate in each individual," so that "[t]he idea of soul can be understood only in relation to the idea of *mana*" (188).

Durkheim's model provides us with the ability to consider the creative process of the artist in ways that the sociology of art has seldom, if ever, considered.

The idea of the soul as a creative principle is certainly something that artists themselves have historically acknowledged along with the idea that art and creativity involve a kind of power or force. Consider, for example, Walt Whitman's (1959 [1855]) well-known poetic invocations in his *Leaves of Grass,* where he writes that "[w]hatever satisfies the soul is truth" or "I believe in you my soul ... the other I am must not abase itself to you/And you must not be abased to the other"; or Wassily Kandinsky's treatise *Concerning the Spiritual in Art* wherein Kandinsky asserts that "the beautiful ... is produced by internal necessity, which springs from the soul" (Kandinsky quoted in Ormond 2003:212). And in characterizing the "force" of artworks, a more contemporary (if less well-known) artist argues that there is an energy inherent in the painting: "We actually receive vibrations from paintings. These vibrations emanate from colors. When we say we receive a charge from a work of art, it is not just psychological in nature. Physical properties are affecting us" (Flack 1986:16). Vincent Van Gogh's plaintive "But when shall I paint my starry sky, that picture which preoccupies me continuously? Alas! Alas!" reflects a certain conception of the artist's creative process that awaits a kind of creative force or power, as reflected in one of Van Gogh's letters to his brother, Theo: "Oh my dear brother, sometimes I know so well what I want. I can do very well without God in my life and my painting, but I cannot, ill as I am, do without something which is greater than I, which is my life—*the power to create*" (Chipp 1968:32 and 35, emphasis mine). And Marcel Duchamp argued that the goal of good art was to shock the viewer somehow and that such shock has a kind of power to it: "All good painters have only about five masterpieces to their name—[works that] have the *force* of shock" (Marquis 2002:275).

The most immediate understanding of creative power or force as a kind of "spiritual" orientation is often related to the idea of inspiration. Artists often *feel* inspiration as a force or form of energy, as the quote from Van Gogh attests. As Willem de Kooning, a well-known abstract expressionist painter, once put it, artists "only want to be inspired." (in Chipp 1968: 560). When Durkheim asserts that the idea of the soul relates to "something divine in us," it can be related to this type of transmittable and external power or force. The famous surrealist René Magritte often spoke of the "mystery" of art. Part of this "mystery" is the unpredictable and often evanescent nature of inspiration, which, as Durkheim says of the soul, is often "that which is best and deepest in ourselves, the pre-eminent portion of our being; and yet it is also a temporary guest that has come to us from the outside, lives an existence in us distinct from that of the body, and must one day reclaim its independence" (188).

In this sense, the production of the artwork to the artist can be likened to the native's relationship to the totem, one of awe and mystery. There is in the creation of the artwork a kind of "participation mystique," or mystical participation, that results in the creation of something seemingly beyond the powers of the artist herself. Duchamp referred to the difference between the artist's original intention and the finished work of art as the "art coefficient." In order for the artist to bring such a work into being, he or she must rely on inspiration as a kind of faith, a "religious" faith, a determination to persevere in creative work despite there being nothing more than the merely "invisible" potential at hand. The traditional idea of "the Muse" involves such an appeal to this higher force. In Dante's *The Divine Comedy*, for example, the author lays out a highly complex poetic rendition of the Roman Catholic conception of the afterlife, but his appeal in writing the great work is not to God but to his own creative muse.

Persistence in art, then, for the artist is much like the "faith" that Durkheim speaks for the Australian aboriginal, in which its true function is to enable the artist to draw on deeper resources to sustain their belief. It can be said of the artist's relationship to art, as Durkheim says of religion, that it is "impervious to experience." Van Gogh's "When will I paint my starry, starry sky?" is a reflection of a "religious" attitude that enables the artist to live and continue in his or her work with a kind of faith in the unknown, the same faith that sustains the "worshipper" whether it be of a god or a work of art: "The worshipper who has communed with his god is not only a man who sees new truths that the unbeliever does not know; *he is a man who is capable of more.* He feels more strength in himself, either to cope with the difficulties of existence or to defeat them" (Durkheim 2001:311–12, emphasis in the original). The "sympathetic vibration" that Durkheim sees between the worshipper and the totem is no less true of the artist and the artwork and with Durkheim we can say that "[o]ur entire study rests on this postulate: that this unanimous feeling of believers across time cannot be purely illusory" (312).

Yet if the idea of the force or power of inspiration can be seen as enabling, it can also be seen as disabling, as with another kind of force: the principle of "resistance." The phenomenologist Jean-Luc Marion (2002) speaks of what he calls "the resistance to the revealed" on the part of the artist, asserting that the struggle of the artist with resistance is a necessary and important part of artistic creation and that, indeed, resistance is productive creatively in that it can ultimately generate the same kind of energy and "heat" as does the resistance to an electrical current.

Durkheim's "religious" model not only is applicable to the creative process whereby the artist creates but also is valid for understanding the ritual practices and beliefs involved in the creative "reception" of art and the artwork by the public or audience. The environment of the movie theater or music concert, for example, generally involves a ritual environment characterized by the kinds of practices Durkheim alludes to in the worship of the totem— the prevalence of darkness, as well as the interplay between darkness and light, the ritual space between the audience and the performers that cordons off the "sacred" from the mundane or profane, the "taboos" involved in certain behaviors relating to the performance, and so forth. Moreover, the music star or movie star is a kind of totemic figure, larger than life and, at least for the duration of the performance, "sacred." In this sense, we can extend Durkheim's model to the idea of something like a "civil religion" of music or film or any other art, where the "cult" is efficacious through its ability to bring the audience together for the purposes of ritually reaffirming the norms and values of the broader society. It is in such ways that modern, differentiated societies compensate for the lack of a more concentrated "collective consciousness" so characteristic of more primitive societies.

In terms of popular art, we can see this "religious" dynamic at work in what Talcott Parsons called the "expressive revolution" of the 1960s, in which songwriters such as Bob Dylan and John Lennon revolutionized popular music through their use of the "confessional" mode of lyric, baring their "souls" in ways that musicians had seldom done before. This confessional mode in turn reflected the energy or power of the 1960s as a historical period generally. The "contagion" that Durkheim speaks of as being so essential to the categories of the sacred and profane may be seen in regard, say, to the release of *Sgt. Pepper's Lonely Hearts Club Band* in June 1967, in which there was a "contagiousness of the sacred"; that is, music fans throughout the world recognized the advent of a "sacred" event in much the same way as today, in a very different context, fans react to the release of the latest Harry Potter book. And today we still identify certain definitive events of the 1960s "cultural revolution" by their residual force or power, such as the Beatlemania of the early 1960s, Bob Dylan's going electric at the Newport Folk Festival, the "scene" at Andy Warhol's "Silver Factory," the Monterey Pop Festival of 1968, and, finally, Woodstock. Each of these events can be seen to embody a kind of "totemic principle" or energy (and therefore cultural power) in terms of character, and they bear a strong similarity to the alternately chaotic and overwhelming forces that Durkheim describes occurring during the Australian aboriginal corroboree.

The immanent model of the soul can perhaps best be related to the idea of creative fertility. In his chapter on "The Notion of the Soul," Durkheim relates certain tribal beliefs among the Australian aboriginals in regard to how women become impregnated with the souls of ancestors that are often believed to reside in certain geographic locations, substances, or otherwise physical entities. This illustrates a deep relationship, mythological relationship between the physical and the spiritual, and the notion that fertility results from a combination of the two. But fertility is not morality. The release of *Sgt. Pepper* and Woodstock can both be seen to have involved a kind of "sacred contagion," but that is not to say that they are of the same order or quality of sacrality. The artist is a "sacred" or "spiritual" figure in contemporary society not merely because he or she has the power or energy to create but also because the artist's creation and creativity is often represented in a *moral* way. As a cultural figure, the artist exemplifies or represents a kind of "moral" conscience.

To consider the moral dimension of artist, we will have to consider Durkheim's other model of the soul.

THE TRANSCENDENT MODEL OF THE SOUL: THE ARTIST AS COLLECTIVE REPRESENTATION

Durkheim argued that all religions consisted of beliefs (ideas) and rites (ritual practices). If the immanent model of the soul deals best with the latter, it is the transcendent model that can best deal with the former. For Durkheim saw the power of the sacred, and therefore the soul, in terms of not only its raw energy or force but its *moral* power. Durkheim will thus state that of the soul that "it is not simply imagined as made of a more subtle and fluid material; but in addition it inspires something of those feelings that are always reserved for the *divine*" (193). The soul for Durkheim is sacred, while the body is profane: "Passion individualizes, yet enslaves." Hence, this second dimension of the artist will relate to a kind of "higher standard," a transcendent ideal. It is in this sense that the figure of the artist has become a significant collective representative of what Durkheim called "the cult of the individual."

In moving from the immanent notion of the idea of the soul as energy or force to the idea of the soul as idea or representation, we move from a phenomenology to a hermeneutic method of analysis. In Durkheim's terms, we go from considering the "totemic principle" as being merely "efficacious" to its being deeply "moral."

"Society can neither create nor recreate itself without at the same time creating an ideal," wrote Durkheim, and the figure of the artist is one such ideal-type, the prototype of a "higher" calling. Artistic practice, for the artist, cannot be reckoned merely in material or empirical terms, it is rather the pursuit of a kind of salvation, the "saving" of one's creative self or soul. This, of course, gets at the "vocational" dimension of art and the artist, who has traditionally been associated with a "school" of work, regardless of the medium: "Art," as one contemporary artist puts it simply, "is a calling" (Flack 1986:3).

If the aim of all religion is salvation, then the aim of inspiration, both religiously and artistically, is revelation. Art, like religion, is a revelatory medium. The artist is, in many ways, seen as a modern prophet, a social actor who lives in the realm of revelation, recognition, and disclosure, one who listens for messages and to whom special messages about reality are disclosed. As Audrey Flack (1986) has written in her *Art and Soul,* "the ultimate achievement [for the artist] is a transference of . . . revelation from private to public" (9).

Art is "religious" and the artist a kind of "worshipper" also with regard to the traditions, myths, and deities that are invoked in regard to the creative process. Durkheim refers to the Alcheringa, or "dreamtime," of the Australian aboriginals, the so-called origin of time during which the ancestral, mythic, larger-than-life figures were said to live and walk the Earth, for sacred beings, Durkheim tells us "are, by definition, separate beings" (221). We can see this same element in any work on a "school" of art or the nearest museum, where every significant art movement is portrayed as having existed in such an "originary" and often "mythical" state. Artworks are thus often seen to be "sacred" relics of such timeless figures. The very idea of the museum is founded on the idea that the profane must not touch the sacred. Every artist is inspired by such prototypical figures and mythic eras. Every artist is inspired to become an artist by some other artist. Moreover, Flack (1986) finds yet another connection between the artist and dreamtime: "The element of time in the creative process is similar to dream time. It stretches and contracts as you work, you can work on something for weeks and weeks and nothing will happen, and yet something can transpire in only an hour. The last five minutes of dream time can process data of epic proportions, and yet one needed the entire night's sleep to arrive at the dream images" (9).

The history of art, whether "high" or "popular," contains any number of such magical, mythical eras, larger-than-life periods of dreamtime. The so-called American Renaissance of the mid–nineteenth century, for example, involving Whitman, Melville, Emerson, and Thoreau, or that of the "second" American Renaissance of the early twentieth century, associated with Alfred Stieglitz and Edward Steichen, among others, is frequently considered in terms of transcendent qualities. Certainly the era of abstract expressionism in the mid–twentieth century, with its "metaphysicians in paint" such as Jackson Pollock, Willem de Kooning, and Barnett Newman, can be seen as a "heroic" era. Even the subsequent advent of pop art has its "religious" overtones as when the art critic Robert Hughes likened Andy Warhol's Factory to a kind of Catholic cult, given that so many of Warhol's hangers-on and assistants came from Catholic backgrounds (Warhol himself regularly attended mass throughout his life). Each of these movements and the artists involved are associated with a certain set of specific cultic rites and rituals, schismatic tendencies and dogma, all of which have some kind of "transcendent" appeal.

It is precisely this transcendent quality or characteristic that constitutes the artist as a "spiritual" figure, a collective representation. The idea of the "life of the artist" involves certain standards and values, which is why what Ralph Waldo Emerson called our "representative men" become a way of understanding ourselves as a society: for, as Emerson also wrote, "properly speaking there is no history, only biography." Artists, then, are not only judged based on their works. Once they become a public or totemic figure and once they produce some kind of recognized oeuvre, artists' life histories inevitably accompany their work and become an intimate and inseparable aspect of the interpretation of that work. Famous artists, because they are artists, may indeed lead a different life from the ordinary citizen, but they may not abstain from accounting for it. But artist biography is also a means of the mythification of the artist—that is, of establishing their "magical" or "religious" stature. As the psychologist Otto Rank has put it: "Biography is as little an objective science as history is, even when it endeavors to be so, and would never fulfill its purpose if it were. The formative process of the biography begins long before the actual attempt to picture the life of the artist; after all, the main purpose is the picture of the creative personality and not merely of the man of actuality, and the two portraits can never be wholly identical" (Rank 1989 [1932]:383).

There is what we might refer to as a "cultural structure of the artist," a set of ritual (for, after all, narrative is a form of ritual) conventions through which we portray the artist as a cultural figure, the "distortions" or "exaggerations" of which have less to do with faulty perception or inaccurate reporting of the actual "facts" or details regarding the artist than with the requirements of collective representation. The "creative effervescence" surrounding the portrayal of the artist in contemporary society springs as much from the structure of the collective consciousness, according to Durkheim's conception of it, as it does from the artist's life itself, for Durkheim writes of the "feelings, ideas and images" that constitute the collective consciousness that "[t]hey are mutually attractive and repellent, they fuse, segment and proliferate without being directly ordered and required to do so by the state of underlying reality" (319).

In their pathbreaking cultural analysis of the "artist myth"—*Legend, Myth and Magic in the Image of the Artist*—Ernst Kris and Otto Kurz (1979 [1934]) offer several biographical motifs or recurring anecdotes that have characterized artist biography (i.e., constituted the genre of the "life of the artist") since Giorgi Vasari's *Lives of the Artists* in the fifteenth century and that still, they claim, appear in contemporary artist biographies:

1. Initial inspiration (encounter with a "master" or masterpiece)
2. The "calling" to art as a vocation (early premonitions of later talent)
3. The self-invention of the person as "artist" (rebirth, new identity)
4. Obscurity/suffering for art (striving for a distinctive style of expression)
5. (a) Discovery of theme (personal) and (b) Recognition of talent (public)
6. Success and fame ("sainthood," achievement, popularity)
7. Fall from grace ("sinfulness," failure, solitude)
8. Late renaissance (usually at lesser stature than peak success)
9. Posthumous acknowledgment (placement within a canon or tradition)

The idea of the art hero arose in Renaissance Italy, Kris and Kurz assert, and the motifs and conventions through which the art hero has been constructed have been remarkably resilient over time. Indeed, the very salience of artist biography is a key indicator to the rise in status of the artist: "in the late Middle Ages, in the fourteenth and fifteenth centuries, when the figure of the artist emerges on the historical scene and gains independent statute in every way, biography of the artist as an independent entity emerges as well" (6). Kris and Kurz argue that what they call the "heroization" and "denigration" of the artist are often accomplished via conventions which stem from earlier Greek myths.

> The vicissitudes of the artist's life, which veer between Parnassus and Montmarte in the representation of the artist's life.... This dual characterization of the artist, at once both admirable and danger-ous, regularly reappears in the traditional accounts and persists in actively shaping the attitudes of his contemporaries to him. (8)

Another scholar has characterized these polar themes as an "optimis-tic" versus a "pessimistic" myth of the artist and their relationship to creativity:

> The *optimistic* tradition is rooted in Greek science and mythology. The protagonist is immortal—he is Hermes, the divine child, who stole the cattle of his brother Apollo on the first day of his life, in-vented the lyre, and gave it to the physician god in atonement.... From the Kabala and the Christian mystical tradition comes ... the view of moments of creation as moments of self-realization, unity with the divine, peak experience.... The mythic prototype of the *pessimistic*, tragic tradition is the poet marked by the gods, inspired by divine madness, taboo to his fellows—blind Homer, Orpheus killed by Maenads, Empedocles the outcast throwing himself into Mount Aetna, rejected Sappho casting herself from the Leucadian rock into the sea. (Mahlendorf 1985:3)

These "optimistic" and "pessimistic" scenarios, the "heroization" and "denigration" of the artist, may be seen in terms of Durkheim's sacred and profane dichotomy, with the optimistic/heroization side of the dichotomy rendering the so-called art hero, while the pessimis-tic/denigration side relates to what we can call the artist's "fall from grace." This "rise and fall" scenario, like the artist biography itself, then, is clearly a ritual structure, a kind of literary "rite of purification" in terms of the artist's image, functioning to align the artist figure with qualities of either purity (fertility) or pollution (decay).

What is significant about the "life of the artist" as a convention is not only that the public understands the artist in terms of this "cultural structure" but that artists understand themselves in the same way. This returns us to Alexander's idea of "subjective structuralism" in the sense that artists, too, requires a template to make sense of their life and creativity and draws on the same cultural resources as their audience, narrative being one of these resources. Durkheim argued that all time was "social time," that the increments through which we measure our lives such as calendars are all provided by society rather than ourselves: "It is not *my* time that is organized this way, but time as it is objectively conceived by everyone in the same civilization" (12). Time is one of the "categories of understanding" that Durkheim sees as structuring our collective life. We might add "narrative" to these categories following philosopher Paul Ricoeur's (1984) contention that time and narrative are always found together: all narratives are about time (in some way), and time is made meaningful or understandable only through narrative. In this way, we can begin to consider how both the artist and the public relate to time or temporality in terms of creativity—and morality. Again, for the purposes of the transcendent conception of the artist, it is not enough that artists be merely "fertile"; they must also have some "higher purpose."

In terms of the narrative/ritual self-understanding of the artist, we can say the heart of the artist lies in the struggle to create, which is rendered via a romance of expression, a variant of the traditional quest narrative. This romance is usually composed of three different dimensions of creativity): (1) the self-invention of the artist persona (Harold Rosenberg: "The artist is someone who has created an artist"); (2) the mastering of a style (artists are defined by their distinctive, and new, style); (3) the creative act (the drama of the artist often related to the physical or embodied pursuit of the artwork) (Sherwood 2002).

At its most basic level, the quest narrative of the artist in pursuit of expression represents what literary theorist Northrop Frye refers to as the "triumph over time," the basic element in all romance wherein some exceptional or remarkable event interrupts and transcends the usually mechanical passage of "dead" time.

The romance of expression is complemented by two other narratives, each of which offers a kind of "profane" or oppositional element to the "sacred" quest of the artist. The first of these is what we might call the "realism of production"; the second is the "irony of embodiment." Both production and embodiment represent the more material, less ideal circumstances out of which artists must somehow conceive their artwork, and each of these counternarratives in some way demonstrates that the artists, in fact, "prisoners" of time and their mortality or, better, corporeality.

Expression, production, and embodiment, then, are the three narrative dimensions through which the ritual "rise" and "fall" of the artist myth is conveyed and out of which the cultural structure of the artist is constructed. The artist biography is invariably rendered as a drama in which the artist's expression is always threatened and often defeated by the needs of production or the impediments of bodily instinct. The "spiritual" character of the artist is always opposed to the temptations of production (e.g., "selling out," "going commercial," etc.) as well as those of the body (e.g., "sex, drugs, and rock 'n' roll"). What is at stake here, in representational terms, is clearly what we can refer to, following Durkheim, as the creative "soul" of the artist.

As the fundamental dynamic in all narrative is transformation, the artist as a moral figure will be rendered through a kind of teleological trajectory—that is, the transformation from a creativity of the immanent variety, represented in Durkheim's model by the corroboree, to the "higher" form embodied by some kind of social movement, for example, such as the ideals of the French Revolution that Durkheim uses to illustrate a more transcendent form of the sacred.

We can see that the career of John Lennon, for example, from cofounder of the Beatles to his shocking assassination, has been retrospectively narrated as a kind of "hero's journey," where Lennon first comes to public consciousness through the force and power of Beatlemania but eventually leaves the Beatles and pursues a second career as the prophetic figure who authors songs such as "Imagine" and "Instant Karma" and engages in social activism for peace, equality, and justice. Lennon goes from being merely a popular entertainer whose fame results from a kind of social density, the fame of celebrity, to a significant and serious "artist" whose art and discourse are represented as emphasizing universalism and idealism. Not to mention the fact that Lennon's use of drugs and a promiscuous lifestyle are represented as having evolved into his being a "happy househusband" to his wife, Yoko Ono, and their child, Sean, at the time of his death. With the publication of Albert Goldman's scandalous *The Lives of Lennon* biography in 1987, Lennon's public image became the subject of great debate in such places as *The New York Review of Books*, *Newsweek*, and *The New Republic* during the late 1980s. Around the same time that Goldman's scathing biography was released, Ono commissioned longtime Hollywood producer David Wolper to make a sympathetic documentary about Lennon entitled *Imagine: John Lennon*. Wolper's documentary, coincidentally, appeared roughly at the same time as Goldman's biography. *Newsweek* wrote of the documentary:

> What [Wolper] is doing is the definitive version of the John Lennon myth. In this familiar saga, John begins as an insouciant but unthreatening teen idol, gets a little weird behind drugs and

Eastern mysticism, goes through a phase where he's going to save the world, bags that and turns party animal and finally settles down to domesticity, even putting his career on hold to become a bread-baking househusband.... This is the myth Yoko Ono wants graven in stone and handed down to posterity. And it's the myth Goldman has blasphemed. (Gates 1988:58)

Newsweek goes on to assert that the battle between Goldman and Ono, Wolper, and others in defining Lennon's life is "a battle not only over the image of John Lennon, but, implicitly, over how a generation sees its own history." In other words, if Lennon is the "fraud" that Goldman makes him out to be, then so are the values, hopes, and aspirations of the baby boom generation that embraced him so fully. As Louis Menand wrote in *The New Republic,* "If there is a lesson to be drawn from the history of the Beatle's celebrity and its press, it might be that informed judgments about the 'real' lives of people like Lennon and McCartney are impossible" (1988:34). The title of Menand's article? "The Lives of the Saints."

Another transformation of this type, from immanent to transcendent, from being less "soulful" to more "soulful," can be seen in an even more culturally ambiguous figure, Andy Warhol. Whereas Lennon might be seen as the quintessential narrator of the artist's life as being a "romance of expression," Warhol predicated his entire career on being what is referred to as an "unreliable narrator" (in Wayne Booth's terms). Warhol's homosexuality, his avowed experimental lifestyle, his cultivation and involvement with an especially "bohemian" fringe during the days of his Silver Factory in the mid-1960s, his rejection of the "romance" of art in any overt form ("Art?" Warhol once remarked, "Isn't that a man's name?")—all would seem to counter the idea of a "higher purpose" in terms of his collective representation. Yet, beginning with the eulogy at his funeral in 1987 by the art critic John Richardson, there has been a concerted effort to provide Warhol with a "soul." Richardson's eulogy challenged the conventional portrait of Warhol and instead painted him as a deeply "devout" man who attended Catholic mass daily, served in soup kitchens, and was even responsible for religious conversion. Since then, a number of articles and books have discussed Warhol's last great creative project, a series of depictions of the Last Supper, offering it as proof of Warhol's deeply spiritual character. The "religious" dimension of Warhol, whether Warhol actually had one or not, has now been posthumously "discovered" and bestowed on Warhol not necessarily out of any intrinsic morality Warhol may have possessed but due to the requirements of collective representation and the "moralizing" impulse that drives them.

CONCLUSION: THE ARTIST AS A RITUAL FIGURE

In applying what Alexander refers to as "the spiritual program of Durkheim's later writings" to the contemporary artist, I believe we can gain new and valuable insights into the artist and the creative process as well as the representation of the artist and what that means for contemporary society. After all, the essence of Durkheim's own insight in the EFRL is that it is not the totem that is itself sacred but the *representation* of the totem—that is, the creative and dynamic forces of society of which it is merely the emblem. In this sense, we might say, after Gaston Bachelard, that the force of the artist lies at least partly in the fact that she is "always dreamed first."

In his work on Durkheim, Alexander (1989) asserts that "Durkheim's sociology ... is about the meaning of structure" (147). The value of Durkheim and Alexander's reappropriation of him are to correct the common misconception both within academia and without that the creative imagination is somehow an individual accomplishment or achievement. The "life" of any artist is not simply a series of random and unconnected images but constructed through emplotment derived from myth. The only access we have to any kind of history or temporality comes not through discrete "facts" but through some kind of story. The romantic, comic, tragic, or ironic artist, then, consists not simply of the random and discrete memories we may have of the artist; these varying forms of emplotment are the fundamental archetypes through which we are able to consider the artist's memory at all. And in a cultural and social sense, these categories only apply to "the artist" because they apply to each of us: they are cultural and social constructions emanating from our core values, norms, and beliefs as a society.

But, again, what generally goes unremarked is that these images are not simply random and unrelated. "The artist," as collective representation, is a cultural and historical figure and therefore an ongoing work of imaginative construction. The cultural imagination, too, has its structures, and the "life of the artist" is one of them. We might say, following Durkheim, that the artist is a story told by society.

Yet the representation or narrative of the artist as a ritual figure is matched by the ritual dimension of the creative process itself. What both of these ritual dimensions share is the "creative force" or energy that Durkheim sees at the heart of society itself. The power of creation, like the power of the collective representation, partakes of the sacred "fire in all things." Inspiration and resistance are very real forces with which all artists contend. The creation of the art work and the labor and sacrifice (of whatever variety) it requires needs to be sufficiently acknowledged. Heretofore, sociologists have almost completely over-looked the creative process as if it were incidental or secondary to the more material considerations—say, race, class, or gender—that the artist must confront. Perhaps this is because these latter dimensions more easily fit the theories and methodologies with which most conventional sociologists work. The significance of considering creativity as a kind of force is that it enables us to broaden such theories and methodologies to meet the artist at least halfway. Within the history of art, the idea of a kind of "soulfulness" as relating to the artist's struggle for authenticity and creativity has a long lineage. It is time for sociology to catch up to what religious and aesthetic discourses have long been able to acknowledge: that the "sacred" is a very real dimension for many artists and the practice of their art.

The response from many within the field of the sociology of art may be that the conception of the artist that I have tried to provide above is too "romantic." Sociology as a narrative, after all, is founded on a kind of "realism," the realism of race, class, and gender being one prominent variant. C. Wright Mills once wrote that the "sociological imagination" lies at the intersection of biography and history. But we have had decades of sociological "realism" and very little by way of either innovation or insight into the beliefs, practices, or rites of the contemporary artist. Sociology's great imperative, the "discovery of society," has for too long obscured modern society's great cultural achievement, which Durkheim referred to as "the cult of the individual." To ignore the "individuals" and their cultural construction is just a great an omission as to unduly favor them. The figure of the artist is a particularly apt representation of the cultic realm of modern individuality.

The poet Wallace Stevens once said that "realism is a corruption of reality." In other words, sociologists should not mistake the sociological imagination for the *only* form of imagination. Sociology's realism can be defined only in relation to more romantic conceptions, and some artists at least, clearly possess such conceptions. The litmus test for a sociology of art should not be what conventional sociology can bear but what effective understandings of the artist require. To that end, I believe the realm of the sacred and the soul as I have outlined them contribute something valuable by way of a *cultural* sociology of the artist.

The cultural imagination has been insufficiently understood by sociology, but the foundation offered by Durkheim's masterwork and its appropriation by Alexander and others offers a potentially valuable resource. That Durkheim's late work should be used as a platform for the exploration of artistic creativity and imagination is no coincidence.

The EFRL itself was not written after years of fieldwork among the Australian aboriginals Durkheim wrote so passionately about, but rather in Durkheim's study tens of thousands of miles away with the aid of the numerous ethnographies Durkheim cites throughout the book. In other words, the EFRL itself was and is a highly effective imaginative accomplishment. Creativity, after all, is an element of all life, and sociology is no exception. Unfortunately, the aesthetic dimension of what sociologists themselves do is itself a largely neglected area of work. It is rather sad that the "sociological imagination" generally acts to obscure deeper consideration of the active cultural imagination of sociologists (Alexander and Sherwood 2002).

To consider the artist as a ritual figure, as I have done here, is to acknowledge the deep importance of tradition. To speak of the cultural structure of the artist in terms of tradition, we can say, along with Ron Eyerman and Andrew Jamison (1998), that "a tradition is both real and imagined at the same time; indeed it is the active identification with a tradition, the conjuring up, the imagining, that makes it real, that literally makes it come to life" (30). In this sense, we might agree with Paul Ricoeur when he writes of the "role of fiction in shaping reality" or with Gaston Bachelard's assertion that "in order to study something one must dream about it first."

For in the end, the "real" artist, like reality itself, is only accessible through the cultural imagination and the traditions it provides. By returning to Durkheim's classic, I have made a modest attempt to explore that vast and infinite realm. Whether I have succeeded or not is less important than the attempt for we can say of the study of the artist what Durkheim long ago said of the study of society: "It is less important to succeed than to dare" (181).

CHAPTER 5

Music as Agency in Beethoven's Vienna

Tia DeNora

The Music Itself?

Musicologists often complain that sociologists consider everything except music itself. They have a point. The body of literature that is sociology of music consists mainly of work on music's social shaping and work devoted to music's role as a signifier of social status and belonging. Very little has dealt with music's role in social ordering.

Posed as part of the growing counter to this trend, this chapter deals with the question of how music is a medium for agency. By *agency*, I mean capacities, modes, and opportunities for action, produced and distributed across individuals that afford preconditions, pretexts, and media for social performance. I use a particular case study of musical life—the reception and performance (at the piano) of Beethoven in early nineteenth-century Vienna—to develop two main themes. The first of these is that music, in conjunction with the frames applied to it, is a medium for modeling role relationships in and/or outside the musical realm. The second, related theme is that the practical, situated, and material performance of music further specifies music's discursive properties. As McCormick (this volume) observes, performance is an all-too-neglected topic in music sociology.

Yet, the focus on music-as-practice (and music-as-performed) highlights the nonverbal, embodied, and otherwise tacit ways in which music may come to be understood as modeling, mediating, or otherwise registering social relations and sensibilities. Performance also illuminates the inevitable incompleteness of musical texts (notations), which, in conjunction with performance practices and performance occasions, come to be understood instead as "scripts"—that is, as implying choreography of, as Cook (2003) observes, "a series of real-time, social interactions between players; a series of mutual acts of listening and communal gestures that enact a particular vision of human society" (206).

Various scholars are now at work on this more symmetrical equation of music society. New modes of enquiry have pursued questions concerning music and the body, music, "health" and well-being, music and conflict resolution, music, place, space and identity, and music's real-time performance. These investigations have, in recent years, been posed and elaborated with some potentially powerful consequences for sociological theories of agency, for the understanding of mind-body issues, and for the better appreciation of the role of the aesthetic in social ordering (Eyerman and Jamieson 1998; Hennion 2001; Juslin and Sloboda 2001; Macdonald, Hargreaves, and Miell 2002; Clayton, Herbert, and Middleton 2003; DeNora 2000; 2003; Ruud 2002; Pavlicevic and Ansdell 2004; Clarke and Cook 2004).

Most of this work has, perhaps naturally, given its empirical and ethnographic nature, dealt with music in relation to current social life. Yet there is no reason why a "how to do things with music" focus may not be applied equally to historical topics; indeed, if we are to comprehend how and why our current musical conventions took shape and provide ordering materials in the ways that they do, we need to consider their histories. With this aim in mind, I turn now to a historical case study, one that, from somewhat different perspectives, I have considered on previous occasions (e.g., DeNora 1995). I will consider the question of how Beethoven and his music, in and through its production, reception, and performance, can be understood to have modeled new modes of agency in and beyond the musical world of Vienna in 1790–1810.

A New Interiority? Beethoven and the Self in Modern Society

In a discussion of Liszt, Richard Leppert (1999) has written:

> For the first time in Western history, the cultural pecking order of the arts was rearranged so that music, formerly judged lesser

than the textual and visual arts, was considered pre-eminent. Music was the sonorous sign of inner life, and inner life was the sign of the bourgeois subject, the much heralded, newly invented, and highly idealized "individual." The European gold standard of the sonorous inner life was quickly and generally established as Beethoven. (253)

There is richness here for music sociology: Music, and in particular the conglomeration of Beethoven and his music, Leppert suggests, provided a point of reference through which the modern idea of the individual and of inner life were developed during the nineteenth century.

This theme has received attention from other music scholars, too, most notably Scott Burnham in his 1995 book *Beethoven Hero*. There, Burnham identifies features of Beethoven's rhetorical compositional style that, he suggests, provided the linchpin around which new images and conventions of various kinds in music came to coalesce—the concept of the "heroic" in music (and the musician as hero), the idea of the powerful and autonomous artist, the notion of the musician as engaged in moral struggle, the idea of music as a quest.

Burnham describes how Beethoven and his music came to be conceived as the "Beethoven Hero," within which Beethoven himself became "the embodiment of music" (xvi), the artist-as-hero who "liberated" music as Burnham puts it, "from the stays of eighteenth-century convention" (xvi). The Beethoven hero notion extends well beyond the works Beethoven composed in his so called heroic style of about 1803–1809; it refers much more broadly to the new ideas of social and psychic agency that Beethoven and his music came to exemplify. These ideas were propounded and elaborated by generations of later composers, from Schumann, who speaks of what he terms Beethoven's "virile power," to Wagner, who wrote on the one hundredth anniversary of Beethoven's birth (1870) of how Beethoven had created music and new purposes of music fundamentally different from his predecessors. If Leppert and Burnham are correct, we should be able to trace this imagery as it was constructed in and around Beethoven's music and to consider how his music came to be constituted as a cultural "work space" (DeNora 1986) through which new conceptions of agency were elaborated.

We may explore this issue from many complementary angles. In what follows I deal with two. The first consists of a focus on discourse. I suggest that the development of the imagery of the Beethoven hero was primed by philosophical and literary critical discussions (Kant's notion of the sublime and Schiller's idea of sentimental art), that these discussions were then extended in musical critical discourse, and, finally, that the notions developed in musical critical discourse were then applied to Beethoven in ways that simultaneously modified both those notions and conceptions of Beethoven and his music. If this argument sounds convoluted, it is because it revolves around the reflexive constitution of, as I have described in earlier work (DeNora 1995), Beethoven and the categories through which he was perceived. Where what I have to say diverges from my earlier work on Beethoven is that I hope to demonstrate how philosophical ideas and their implications for the imagery of agency were recast through discussions of Beethoven's music as opportunities, stances, and postures of action.

The second angle deals with how the discourses associated with Beethoven came to be embodied and thus further specified and elaborated via that embodiment, in and through the performance of Beethoven's works, viewed in context of the culture of performance more widely conceived. In this respect, the topics covered may be read as interacting and exemplifying some of the points made elsewhere in this volume, in particular, McCormick's schematic conception of "music as social performance."

DISCURSIVE DEPICTIONS OF THE BEETHOVEN HERO

The Discourse of "Inner Life" Transposed from Letters to Tones

The idea of "inner life" and its external manifestation as individual agency took shape initially during the 1790s in philosophy, through Kant's notion of the sublime. As elaborated in the *Critique of Judgement* (1790) (for excerpts relevant to music, see translations in le Huray and Day 1981), Kant's notion possessed two important dimensions.

On the one hand, the sublime was mathematical, abstract, and linked to the infinite in its incomprehensibility. On the other hand, the sublime was dynamic; it was a *mental* (indeed, emotional) state, inspired by fear, in particular the fear instilled by natural phenomena (Kant offers examples such as volcanoes and thunder). And it was in and through this dynamic state that self-awareness, according to Kant, was constituted. The apprehension of sublime phenomena, he said, "allows us to discover in ourselves a capacity of resistance.... So sublimity is contained, not in any natural object, but in our mind and spirit, in so far as we can become aware of being superior to nature in ourselves, and thereby to nature outside of ourselves as well" (quoted in Webster 1997:59).

It is here that we see the germ of something new, typically hailed as the Enlightenment notion of human supremacy over nature and with it the idea of the self-reflexive agent. The Kantian sublime provided a vehicle through which the self-conscious and self-empowering individual could be elaborated. The apprehension of the sublime, in other words, led to self-awareness; it posed a relationship between nature (objective, external forces) and the subjective experience of nature (e.g., fear), and, through that experience, *freedom,* understood as the capacity for intervening and so resisting nature.[1]

This idea of "inner life" and its connection to a new and empowered form of agency was developed as an aesthetic theory by Friedrich Schiller in his 1795 discussion of "naive" versus "sentimental" art. There, Schiller posed a distinction between poetry that describes objects and the natural world from which it is not alienated (naive poetry) and poetry about the impressions objects make on the poet and thus, about the realm of the subjective ("inner life"). During the years between roughly 1801 and 1810, these notions were introduced to musical discourse, as other scholars have already shown (Webster 1997; Senner 1999).

In an article first published in 1801 and reissued more widely in 1805 in the *Berlinische Musikalische Zeitung,* the critic C. F. Michaelis described how music could depict the sublime and so arouse the feeling of awe associated with sublimity or how it could depict the subjective experience of feeling in the presence of the sublime:

> Music can either seek to arouse the feeling of sublimity through an inner structure that is independent of any emotional expression, or portray the state of mind aroused by such a feeling. In the first case the music can objectively be called sublime, like untamed nature, which arouses sublime emotions; in the second case, the music portrays what is pathetically sublime. The former resembles epic poetry; the latter lyric poetry. (translated and quoted in Webster 1997:62)

Here we see an early version of the notion that music could not only function programmatically, depicting natural phenomena, but that it could also provide analogues of subjective experience in the face of those phenomena—feelings of terror, awe, and longing, for example.

This idea was given further impetus in the same issue of the *Berlinische Muskalische Zeitung* in a second essay (by an author listed only as C. F. [Michaelis's first initials were C. F.—could it have been he?]). The writer says, "The composer can represent the subjective:

the expression of sensations and emotions, affects and passions.... This kind [of music] one can call lyrical. It is the expression of feeling, full of dominating subjectivity. It is not just beautiful, it is also moving" (quoted in Senner 1999:32).

How, then, was the musical sublime configured? In his essay, Michaelis points to musical devices such as

> long, majestic, weighty, or solemn notes ... long pauses holding up the progress of the melodic line, or which impede the shaping of a melody ... too much diversity, as when innumerable impressions succeed one another too rapidly and the mind is too abruptly hurled into the thundering torrent of sounds, or when ... themes are developed together in so complex a manner that the imagination cannot easily and calmly integrate the diverse ideas into a coherent whole without strain. (quoted in Webster 1997:62–63)

How, then, did these discussions square with Beethoven and his music? Thanks to work by Robin Wallace (1986) and William Senner (1999), it is possible to trace this development by reviewing the ways in which Beethoven's work was discussed and how the terms of that discussion modulated over time. These issues become clear if we focus on Beethoven's reception in the pages of the Leipzig *Allgemeine Musicalische Zeitung* (AMZ), the first journal to review Beethoven's work (it carried a review of early Beethoven works in its first issue in 1798) and the one in which his works were most systematically reviewed.

Reconfiguring Beethoven/Reconfiguring Critical Discourse

Beethoven fared poorly in the earliest issues of the AMZ. He is described, for example, in 1799 as, piling "one thought wildly upon another, and, in a rather bizarre manner, to group them in such as way that not infrequently an obscure artificiality or an artificial obscurity is produced" (Wallace 1986:8, describing the Piano Sonatas op. 10).[2] By 1802, however, after a barbed letter to the editor from Beethoven, in which he threatened to withhold his works from the journal's parent company, a music publisher, should his treatment at the hands of the reviewers not improve ("advise your critics to exercise more care and good sense"), Beethoven is viewed in a more favorable, albeit still preromantic, light in a review of the Violin Sonatas op. 23 and 24: "The original, fiery, and intrepid spirit of this composer, which even in his early works could not escape the attention of astute observers, but which did not always find the most cordial reception, probably because it sometimes sprang forth in a manner that was ungracious, impetuous, dismal and opaque … is now becoming ever clearer" (quoted in Wallace 1986:9).

This discursive process moved from initial hostility to Beethoven, to a slightly begrudging recognition of his "original" talent, to, eventually, depictions of the composer as hero and of the psychological intensity associated with the confrontation of the sublime. In this respect, the transposition of Kant's sublime into musical terms provided a useful resource with which to rehabilitate Beethoven. As Senner (1999) has so astutely observed, "in spite of Kant's intent to promote the public use of reason and his exclusion of music from his philosophy, his advocacy of the aesthetics of productive imagination and the autonomy of art provided the foundation for a view of art that Beethoven's contemporaries could use to attack his Enlightenment opponents" (15).

Accordingly, we see reference to the sublime and its musical construction taking shape in the pages of AMZ between roughly 1801 (the initial publication of Michaelis's essay) and 1805 when, in a review of the C-minor Piano Concerto no. 3, a critic wrote:

> The ever-growing intensity over 32 measures [achieved by drawing out the harmonic progress] … grips the listener irresistibly Beethoven produces a similar effect in the places where, traversing one or more octaves, usually in chromatic scales, he arrives again at the minor 7th or 9th with which the main theme begins, without, however, letting the listener come to rest, but holding him in tension until the theme is stated in its entirety. (Wallace 1986:15)

We begin to see here some of the ways in which Beethoven's music came to be seen as "holding" the listener in train to a new and psychologically charged psychoacoustical landscape, one in which restlessness, suspense, and shock had come to replace melodic and harmonic flow. As one contemporary, the composer Johann Wenzel Tomashek, put it upon hearing Beethoven improvise, "Not infrequently, the unsuspecting listener is jolted violently out of his state of joyful transports" (quoted in Landon 1970:104). Through the ways in which this "violent jolting" was paired with textual descriptions of its meaning, new habits of musical response, associated with new modes of psychic energy and resolve, were posed as opportunities for experience.

By 1810, the critical discourse of romanticism is fully unfurled in Beethoven's honor, illustrated most notably in E. T. A. Hoffmann's famous AMZ review of the Fifth Symphony. There, the idea of "inner life," musically configured, had fully arrived, proffered as the cornerstone of a new, "romantic" aesthetic of autonomous art and defined, above all, by "interminable longing" and, tellingly, by the idea of being able to triumph over ("resist") nature. Hoffman associated romanticism most closely with the medium of instrumental music,[3] which he saw as "scorning every aid, every admixture of another art, [it] expresses the pure essence of this particular art alone" (Senner 1999: 17). Of Beethoven, he wrote, "Beethoven sets in motion the machinery of awe, of fear, of pain" (quoted in Burnham 2000:275). And:

> Now Beethoven's instrumental music opens to us the realm of the colossal and the immeasurable. Glowing beams of light shoot through the deep night of this realm and we perceive shadows surging back and forth, closer and closer around us, destroying everything in us except the pain of that endless longing in which each joy that had risen in jubilant tones sinks back and perishes; and it is in this pain ... which seeks to break our breast with the chords of all the passions that we live on and become enchanted visionaries. (Wallace 1986:21)

Music's Actors—Implied Personae

In the space of little more than a decade, between 1799 and 1810, the German-language critical discourse aligned the idea of the sublime and Beethoven's music in ways that constituted a sea change in musical life. This change was characterized by two key features. First, as music's subject matter shifted to the unfathomable, the tumultuous, the terrifying and, adjacent to this, music was increasingly understood as able to depict "inner life"—fear, awe, yearning, and resistance, music modeled the ideas of psychological interiority, individualism, and the capacity to resist and strive (freedom).

Second, insofar as music came to be seen as providing the best medium for depicting the sublime, the musician—Beethoven—came to be modeled also in new ways, as a heroic, and therefore high-status, actor. It is here that we begin to glimpse the ways that the romantic aesthetic came to be linked to social exclusion, widening gulf between serious and popular taste and between artist and society, a point recognized early on by Schiller himself when he speaks in his 1795 essay of how the sentimental artist is inevitably alienated from the general public by virtue of his attempts to access the infinite (Senner 1999:15).

Similarly, Burnham (2000) describes how Hoffmann "helped create a situation rare in music history: the little understood works of a still living composer were accepted on faith as masterpieces of organic conception and sublime revelation, each held together by a deep and mysterious continuity which, in Hoffmann's words, 'speaks only from spirit to spirit'" (275–76). The new musical materials were (and this is a critical point) *simultaneously* both by-products of and resources for two forms of agency understood as capacity for action: (1) Beethoven's composition of *himself* as a new type of agent with new forms of entitlement and opportunity (a role that Beethoven assumed in an exclusive manner) and (2) the emergence of the critic as a high(er) status intermediary between composer and public.

On the first of these new roles, Beethoven was undoubtedly active in the process of producing himself as a new type of creative agent, one able to conjure forth in music "the colossal and the immeasurable" (quoted in Wallace 1986:21), whose grappling with tumultuous musical issues on an epic scale was able to prove himself as a musical "master." Such a being came to be treated as one who could command attention, one to whom devotion (in the form of silent respectful listening) was due (on changes in the culture of listening, see DeNora 1995; Johnson 1995). "I do not play for such swine," Beethoven notoriously exclaimed in 1802 (Thayer 1967:307), when one of his salon performances was met with less than rapt attention, and in so doing he marked the moment when the balance of authority between patron and musician had begun to shift—again with Beethoven as the linchpin—in favor of the latter.

In short, the Beethoven hero was an extraordinary individual, a "prince of music" as he once described himself to his patron, Prince Lichnowsky. As such, the role Beethoven assumed as a musician and a "master" of music, provided a model for a second, more generalized (and more aspirational) form of agency, the exemplary self, possessed of an ability to, in Kant's terms, "become aware of being superior to nature in ourselves, and thereby to nature outside of ourselves as well" (Webster 1997:59) ().

In sum, music, particularly instrumental music, provided the medium par excellence for the representation of the sublime, and, related to this, it represented "inner" experience. In this sense, Beethoven's musical innovations can be understood to have provided new resources for the configuration of subjective experience; they modeled that experience through the temporal medium of tones. Related to music's new role, new forms of social and psychic agency were also modeled, for both musicians and listeners. Through the ways in which the musician (Beethoven) could be seen to "grapple" with musical material, he became heroic, and, by channeling his listeners' energies, he was simultaneously repositioned in relation to his listeners over whom he came to be seen as having power, through the ways he could command and hold attention, and evoke terror and awe.

FROM DISCOURSE TO PRACTICE

So far, I have dealt with musical experience framed through the pairing of philosophical notions, musical forms, and musical-critical texts. I have yet to consider how Beethoven's music was also made meaningful in and through practical performance—my second aim in this chapter. It is here that questions about how the mediating role of performance as situated activity and as, in this volume, McCormick terms "social performance" is constitutive in its own right of the cultural structures that provide resources for and thereby mediate action.

How and to what extent is it possible to explore these forms of agency as they came to be *enacted* in the milieu of Beethoven's Vienna? And to what extent did the enactment of this agency further elaborate these possibilities and their meanings—how, for example, was the Beethoven imago further specified in and through the how, who, what, when, and where of musical performance practice? I suggest there is much to learn in this regard by moving beyond the level of the cultural analysis of musical texts and their social meanings to consider how these texts came to be performed. Accordingly, in the next section I examine Beethoven's instrumental music as it was performed between 1792 and 1810.

Musical Bodies

At a time when all music was performed live, musical performance was always, and at least implicitly, a visually dramatic event, one that inevitably involved bodily procedures, strictures about comportment, and, at times, choreography. To speak of these matters is to deconstruct the technical neutrality of musical performance and to recognize, by contrast, how musical performance may itself provide significant factors in the overall understanding of works and their perceived meanings. Here, I mean much more than mere phrasing. I mean the performance of performance, the ways in which that music may make demands on the body and how music may be used by performers for embodied display. In these respects, music performance is dramaturgical: the practices of performing may delineate various meanings.

Circa 1800, there was probably no realm within musical performance as charged with social meaning as the keyboard. The piano in late eighteenth- and early nineteenth-century Vienna was at the heart of debates over aesthetic practice, a site at which new and often-competing aesthetics were deployed and defended, at times through the overt medium of the "piano duel" (DeNora 1995:chap. 7). In what ways, then, did the demands made by Beethoven's piano works on the piano-performing body serve to highlight the keyboard artist as a particular type of actor? How, in other words, were the models provided by Beethoven's music further delineated in and through the embodied and visual display associated with their performance? For example, how did musical performance further specify notions about heroic action—more specifically, the embodied lineaments of that action? Who came to be cast as Beethovenian performers? And, equally relevant, who did not? For not all musicians, it would appear, were equally entitled to take up the opportunities for musical action offered by Beethoven's works.

"The Ladies Do Not Wish to Play"

In 1796, Frau Bernard described in her diary how her piano teacher, Andreas Streicher, introduced her to Beethoven's recently published Sonatas op. 2: "One day Streicher put some things by Beethoven in front of [me]; they were the piano sonatas opus 2 which had just appeared at Artaria's [c. 1796]. He told [me] that *there are some new things in them which the ladies do not wish to play* because they are incomprehensible and too difficult, would [I] like to learn them?" (Landon 1976–80:IV:67, emphasis added).

I have described elsewhere (DeNora 2004) how Streicher was probably correct in his assessment that the "ladies did not wish to play" Beethoven. Between 1793 and 1810—at which time Beethoven was perhaps the most frequently performed composer for fortepiano in Vienna—Beethoven's works were performed most often by men: 79 percent of performances of *all* his piano works were performed by men and 21 percent by women, and 84 percent of his concertos by men. Put the other way round, only 16 percent of Beethoven's concerto's were performed by women. This percentage contrasts dramatically with the proportion of male performances of Mozart: 26 percent of *all* his piano works were given by men and 74 percent by women; 27 percent of his concertos were performed by men during 1787–1810 and 73 percent by women.[4]

Between 1803 and 1810, the number of performances of Beethoven's concertos was increasing. Also growing were the number of performers apart from Beethoven who played his concertos (particularly after he retreated from performing them himself as his hearing failed). Yet women continued to be active (Josepha Auernhammer,

Frauline Kurzbeck, Baroness Ertmann, Countess Anna Marie Erdody, and others were all featured on the concert stage during these years). Indeed, women would appear to have given as many and sometimes more performances of piano concertos than men did. However, there is no extant evidence of a female performance of a Beethoven concerto after 1806, a time during which men increasingly took up his works. Once a concerto was published, Beethoven tended not to perform it again himself, and, as his hearing worsened, he entrusted the performance of his works to others. Never before had women and men been divided within the piano repertory in this way.[5]

In other work (DeNora 2004), I have considered why women seem to have been so conspicuously absent from performing what were, arguably, the most prestigious works in the keyboard repertory at a time when they continued to play the concertos of other composers. I have suggested that this gender segregation in the repertory marked the beginning of the women's exclusion from the heart of the musical canon and from the emerging notion of "serious" music during these years.[6]

I have also suggested that it was physical and performative features required and implied by Beethoven's works, and the ways that these features clashed with conventions and mores concerning pianistic display that made the highly public performance of Beethoven (exacerbated by the figure/ground nature of concertos) difficult for women. To understand this issue, it is necessary to contextualize it in terms of who played which instrument, circa 1790.

In the 1780s and 1790s, the keyboard was the predominant instrument for quasi-professional musicians and for aristocratic musical amateurs. For the latter, the allure of the keyboard instrument lay in two features: First, it was an expensive instrument, one that was also physically conspicuous. Second, it permitted a display of embodiment, musically conceived, that was commensurate with, in the 1780s, aristocratic ideals of comportment and bodily display, ideals outlined in 1796 by Frau Bernard's teacher, Andreus Streicher, in his *Handbook for Piano Care and Good Musicianship*. Streicher described the ideal piano-performing body as unobtrusive, self-effacing, one in which all traces of physical and technical effort were suppressed. Just as, in the contemporary phrase of the 1780s, music should "flow like oil" (i.e., tones equally matched so as to create a smooth surface—the analogy was matched pearls, the jewel most worn by Vienna's aristocrats), so, too, Streicher tells us that the good pianist plays in a manner such that "no one is even aware of the artistry."

This quiet body was a vehicle for the display of aristocratic composure and, as such, was commensurate with the favored dance forms of aristocrats during these years—the minuet, for example. Circa 1796 in Vienna, to be an active, overtly physical, musical body was considered lower status—aristocrats simply did not play the types of instruments that called for puffing or puffed cheeks or that involved spittle.

For women, this type of bodily composure was doubly important. To engage in too overtly physical a form of musical display compromised social status but, additionally, femininity and propriety. Thus, circa 1796, the confluence of aristocratic and gender ideologies applied to music rendered male and female bodies at the keyboard equally equipped and equally matched.

It is in this context that we need to consider Beethoven's music in terms of the demands it makes on the pianist's body. Beethoven's music, particularly the devices it employs to represent the sublime (thundering chords, double octaves, sudden and surprising motifs), reinscribes the performing body in terms of its display in ways that brings the pianist's body into sharp visual relief, made most apparent in the concerto genre, when the soloist's body is featured in front of an orchestral backdrop. The embodied techniques featured in Beethoven's music supplanted the aristocratic body with something new, a more dashing, visceral, and energetic body. Beethoven's music can, in other words, be understood to have renegotiated the aesthetics of the body, in ways that downgraded aristocratic values and replaced them with the materiality of visibility of the productive and active musical body.

The mannerisms and gestures associated with Beethoven's music are precisely those that Streicher denigrates in his discussion of the "bad" pianist (or "keyboard strangler"), the player

> of whom it is reputed, "he plays extraordinarily such as you have never heard before." ... Through the movement of his body, arms and hands, he seemingly wants to make us understand how difficult is the work he has undertaken. He carries on in a fiery manner and treats his instrument like a man who, bent on revenge, has his arch-enemy in his hands and, with cruel relish, wants to torture him slowly to death.... He pounds so hard that suddenly the maltreated strings go out of tune, several fly in the direction of bystanders who hurriedly move back in order to protect their eyes.... But why ... does the player have such an obstinate instrument that it will only obey his fingers and not his gesticulations? ... His playing resembles a script which has been smeared before the ink is dried. (quoted in Jones 1999:4, emphasis Streicher's)

As the period-instrument maker and piano historian Margaret Hood (1986) has observed, "Some of the mannerisms [Streicher] ridiculed characterized Beethoven's aggressive and dramatic style of playing" (I:4). Streicher's manual was published in 1796, on the cusp of Beethoven's rising fame. Indeed, it is in the same year that Beethoven initiated his campaign for piano-technological change. He wrote to Streicher from his concert tour in Pressburg, to thank Streicher for the loan of an instrument while on tour (see DeNora 1995:176), "I received the day before yesterday your fortepiano, which is really an excellent instrument.... It is far too good for me ... because it robs me of the freedom to produce my own tone." And again, later in the same year: "The pianoforte is still the least studied and developed of all instruments.... I hope that the time will come when the harp and the pianoforte will be treated as two entirely different instruments." Hood speculates that it was perhaps because of the shifting tide of musical fashion, particularly Beethoven's rapidly rising star, that Streicher's pamphlet was only briefly in circulation.

Beethoven's Bodies

In terms how it is to be performed, Beethoven's music made new demands on the piano-performing body—it required a more visceral keyboard approach and more demonstrative physical action (the choreography associated with this action was even lampooned as the century progressed). These characteristics were not compatible with late eighteenth-century piano technology, and they were in opposition to strictures about appropriate feminine comportment—whether at the piano or elsewhere.

At least in part, the new pianist inscribed in Beethoven's music was Beethoven himself. Observations from his contemporaries suggest his pianistic style was strenuous (DeNora 1995:chaps. 6, 7, and 8). The Beethoven biographer A. W. Thayer has speculated that this visceral approach may have been the result of "all the hardness and heaviness of manipulation caused by his devotion to the organ" (Thayer 1967: I:160) (an instrument that, during the 1780s when Beethoven was active in Bonn as court organist, required a degree of strength far greater than that required by the fortepiano).

At the same time, the body configured in Beethoven's works and in the performance of his works was not reducible to Beethoven's body. True, Beethoven may be understood to have inscribed his body into his music. But so, too, his music came to provide the standard against which his embodied traits then came to be perceived and hailed as insignia of his (and subsequent musicians') genius.

It is here that we see most clearly the reflexive relationship between Beethoven's visceral piano style and the image of the Beethoven hero. The mutual referencing of these two things in turn illustrated the new image of the individual in terms of its opportunities for embodied—and symbolically embodied—action. "Full of vitality, a picture of strength," said Ignaz Seyfried, circa 1820 (quoted in Wegeler and Ries 1987:14) of Beethoven. He became known for his sudden and unpredictable and impulsive behavior—his "raptus," as he and his circle termed it (the tendency to shift impulsively to a preoccupation when overtaken by an idea or inspiration) and his short temper. These characteristics—Beethoven's dynamism—came to be seen as further evidence of his exceptional identity and abilities, his genius.

The musical depiction of "inner life" and its outer correlate of heroic action can be understood to have been delineated not only through musical material but, simultaneously, through the physical practices of its performance that gave rise to a visual imagery of heroic action, musically configured. And it is here that we start to see how music, in and through its performance/enactment, provides object lessons in how to be an agent. In this case, it provided a vocabulary of gestures and a compendium of movement styles associated with powerful individualism. Speaking of how music in the nineteenth century came to involve a "look" as well as sonority, Richard Leppert (1999) observes that, "more than ever before, performers' bodies, in the act of realizing music, also helped to transliterate musical sound into musical meaning by means of the sight—and sometimes spectacle—of their gestures, facial expressions and general physicality" (255; see also Leppert 1993).

During these years in Vienna, similar images were being forged and developed in the scientific and pseudoscientific cultures of physiognomy and Mesmerism (Lavater, the father of physiognomy, continued to promote Mesmer's ideas long after Mesmer himself was forced to leave Vienna, after a scandal involving one of his patients, the pianist Maria Theresa Paradis). There, it is possible to see the gendered notions of capacity for the sublime, heroism, and the rapt or captive audience also being developed and resonating with musical culture. As in music, the notion that special qualities of individuals were locatable in the physical and/or psychological traits of that individual was a concept that inevitably cut across more democratic ideas of talent and meritocracy.

CONCLUSION

As it came to be elaborated in and through musical performance practices, the Beethoven imago was associated with an imagery initially forged in philosophy and aesthetics, and elaborated via bodily performance. That imagery and its musical enactment in turn forged new ideas about the connections between appearance and social capacity, with configurations of social agency. The opportunities to inhabit these configurations were differentially distributed along gendered lines in ways that were consequential for then-emerging conceptions of gender and sexual difference, for masculinity as well as femininity. Further research on performance occasions, revisions to scores in anticipation of those occasions, and reports of performance practices (and their social distribution) will further enrich our understanding of how performance—in this case in the Vienna of Beethoven— helped sketch or script possibilities for social relation and action.[7]

This gender divide widened over the course of the nineteenth century and throughout Europe. Music, in and through its practice, provided object lessons in gender-linked modes of agency. The new forms of musical display, and the agencies they implied, not only excluded women from the heart of the musical canon; they also celebrated a currency of bodily capital (appearance, physique, comportment, and temperament) that was differentially distributed to men. The "freedom" to strive, it would appear, was not readily available to all as, increasingly in music, appearance mattered.

NOTES

1. We see Beethoven employing this discourse of resistance, indeed dramatizing himself as a kind of sublime actor on numerous occasions in his letters. For example, in the famous letter of November 16, 1801, in which Beethoven speaks to his friend Franz Wegeler, he describes how "I will seize Fate by the throat; it shall certainly not bend and crush me completely.... I am no longer suited to the quiet life" (Anderson 1961:68 as quoted in Downs 1970:586).

2. Compare this to Michaelis's description of the musical corollaries of the sublime, quoted earlier and initially published in 1801 ("too much diversity, as when innumerable impressions succeed one another too rapidly").

3. "[Music] is the most romantic of all the arts—one might say, the only purely Romantic art" (quoted in Senner 1999:17). The essay appeared in the preeminent music journal of the day, the Leipzig *Allgemeine Musikalische Zeitung.*

4. The four female performances of Beethoven concertos are given over a one-year period, between 1801 and 1802 (three by Josepha Auernhammer and one by a Miss Stummer, about whom nothing else is known—perhaps she visited Vienna only briefly) and one performance in 1806.

5. Of course, Mozart wrote some of his concertos for his own performance, whereas he wrote others for his female students, but during these years, the women who performed Mozart concertos were not by any means restricted in terms of their access to Mozart's works.

6. For discussions of the gendered character of the musical canon in the nineteenth century and beyond, see Ellis (1997), Citron (1993), McClary (1991), Solie (1993).

7. Ongoing work at Exeter is examining these issues through a collaboration between myself and a musicologist, Timothy Jones, who is a specialist in, among other things, the study of Mozart's concerto autograph scores.

CHAPTER 6

Music as Social Performance

Lisa McCormick

A troubling accusation was recently leveled against the field of musicology: "Because they think of performance as in essence the reproduction of a text, musicologists don't understand music as a performing art" (Cook 2003:204). If the source of this fundamental misunderstanding is the preoccupation with the reproduction of texts, then sociology should fare better in this respect, having long ago rejected a text-based analysis of music. Leaving the "decoding" of artworks to the humanities, sociologists since Adorno have turned their attention instead to the production and use of music in social contexts. Yet, despite their alternative focus, sociologists are guilty of the same charge. They, too, fail to understand music as a performing art. The source of sociologists' misunderstanding of music, however, is the predominance of the economic framework that has defined research in the sociology of the arts since the 1970s: the production/consumption paradigm. By misconstruing music as an object produced by an industry, or used as a resource for social action, sociology has shackled itself to a theoretical vocabulary that, like musicological language, "leads us to construct the process of performance as supplementary to the product that occasions it" (Cook 2003:205). This is not merely an aesthetic issue of marginal importance to sociology's concerns. Understanding music as performance "means to see it as an irreducibly social phenomenon, even when only a single individual is involved"

(Cook 2003:206). Therefore, after Cook, I would like to level my own accusation: Because they think of performance as in essence the final stage of production, sociologists not only fail to understand music as a performing art but also fail to understand music as a social performance.

By *social performance,* I am referring to the "social process by which actors, individually or in concert, display for others the meaning of their social situation" (Alexander 2004:529). The social performance of meaning is typically (and most effectively) communicated within the structure of a ritual. Here, we understand ritual in an anthropological sense, as "episodes of repeated and simplified cultural communication in which the direct partners to a social interaction, and those observing it, share a mutual belief in the descriptive and prescriptive validity of the communication's symbolic contents" (Alexander 2004:527). A defining feature of contemporary societies, however, is the displacement and reflexivity of ritual processes. While ritual-like activities abound, these have become more open-ended in structure. With the increasing complexity and fragmentation of society, the intentions of performers cannot be taken for granted, the meanings performed become ambiguous and open to interpretation, and mutual belief becomes less common and more fragile. This makes cultural communication difficult, but not impossible. Effective social performances are those that succeed in "fusing" together the six elements of performance: systems of collective representations, actors, observers/audience, means of symbolic production, mise-en-scène, and social power (Alexander 2004). If these elements remain uncoupled, or "de-fused," the social performance comes off as contrived and unconvincing. Essentially, it becomes an "empty ritual."

For students of culture, the attraction of performance theory is that it transcends the long-standing divide between structuralist and pragmatist theories of meaning. In my view, the study of music has been similarly divided, but along disciplinary lines. As already mentioned, musicology has primarily defined music as a text, insisting that its meaning derives from its structural properties. In contrast, sociology has insisted that musical meaning is not inherent in the artwork or "music itself" but instead that it emerges from the contingent situation of its production or reception; typically, power and material interest are identified as the most important determinants of meaning. Neither of these positions is completely satisfying. It is only through a multidimensional framework that we can meaningfully integrate text (the "music itself"), context (the contingent situation of music's production or consumption), and action (the situated act of performing and interpreting meaning) in our analysis. It is for this reason I suggest that we consider musical performance as a mode of social performance, a ritual-like activity in the sense described earlier.

The purpose of this chapter is to outline a "performance perspective" for the sociology of music. To begin, I will show how the elements of social performance apply to the field of music, providing some empirical examples for illustration. Although most of my examples will involve classical music, I believe the approach offers insight into all styles of music and all its forms—mediated or live, spontaneous or rehearsed, commercial or amateur, formal or informal—without specifying any form as pure or ideal. To conclude, I will offer a critique of the dominant perspectives within the production/consumption paradigm and suggest how a performative turn would overcome these limitations.

AN OUTLINE OF THE PERFORMANCE PERSPECTIVE

The Layered System of Collective Representations

Every social performance involves a script—premeditated, improvised, or attributed—that draws on shared background symbols and meanings in order to be both intelligible and meaningful in the manner intended by the author. In musical performance, scripts are the musical texts brought to life by musicians. Musical texts can be written down in the form of a notated score, conveyed orally and preserved in memory, or some combination of the two. As the various analytical methods of musicology and ethnomusicology have endeavored to identify, musical texts make use of a considerable repertoire of genres, forms, techniques, and figures that are meaningful because they draw from a shared *musical* system of collective representations. In this way, even instrumental music can carry meaning through its use of the "musical vernacular." It is at this level that the performance perspective can incorporate the methods of the humanities in order to understand how the properties of musical materials shape the meanings communicated in musical performance.

The typical sociological objection to musicological methods and music criticism is to question the extent to which the musical system of collective representations is actually shared within a society. No doubt this charge is motivated in part by "perceived technical inadequacies" on the part of sociologists themselves (Martin 2002:131). While I would caution against confusing knowledge of background musical symbols with proficiency in the academic language developed to analyze them, it remains a difficult, if not impossible, task to acquire the necessary empirical evidence to settle the matter. This has provoked many sociologists to dismiss musicological analysis as ideological discourse, as we have seen in countless acute critiques of Adorno. While denying musicology's truth claims, this position does not deny musicology's status as a background cultural system that informs musical experience, but it does insist that this discourse creates and sustains stratification by disguising metaphor and interpretation as natural and inherent in music's own properties. The "new musicology" of Susan McClary, Philip Brett, and others has shared this critical sensibility, but rather than dismiss the tools of musicology as ideology, they have used those tools to demonstrate how "purely musical" collective representations resonate with other cultural structures or theoretical narratives, such as gender, modern conceptions of selfhood, and the alienation of the subject in modernity. (See, for example, McClary 2000.) This is the more promising position of the two. The tools of formal musical analysis should not be so easily cast aside. Without them, the aesthetic nature of music becomes a black box that sociology must either dismiss as irrelevant or admit lies beyond its explanatory reach.

The musical text, however, displays only the first level of meaning systems informing musical performance. What has never been adequately explored, in my opinion, is the second layer of representations, the background structures that inform the actual *performance* of musical texts. For example, on a very general level, our experience of musical activity is informed by the public/private structure that orders a great deal of our social life. Music is differently performed and differently experienced in a public space such as a concert hall, compared with the personal musical practices enacted in private, such as in the home or in the car. The specific context of musical performance can also invite symbols, metaphors, and structures seemingly unrelated to music. For example, the music competition, organized in the form of a tournament and introducing a rank order of performers, easily lends itself to sports metaphors. The Calgary International Organ Competition, referred to as the "Organ Olympics" by competitors and press alike, is hardly an isolated case.

Myths are another set of symbolic structures informing musical performance. In classical music, the most prominent myths are romantic legacies: music as a universal language, the musical career as a vocation, the timelessness of aesthetic beauty, the uncompromising artist in the face of unsympathetic critics or political opposition. Myths provide the narrative genres and tropes that inform the biography of artistic careers (see Sherwood, this volume) or provide a meaningful context for the interpretation of a particular performance or a specific piece of music. They are populated by the "stock characters" of the music world, icons of performance that actors attempt to embody through their own musical performance. In classical music, these include the child prodigy, the technical virtuoso, the diva, the misunderstood genius, and the temperamental artiste. The most famous myths take place in sacred places that lend symbolic weight to future performances. For classical music, the list would include Vienna, Bayreuth, and Carnegie Hall,[1] while punk music would point to CBGB[2] and rock 'n' roll to Abbey Road. Not all background symbols are of equal significance to both actors and audience, or of equal importance to every segment of the audience. Neither are they necessarily of equal salience in every performance context. My point is simply that the webs of meaning in which musical performance is embedded are multiple and vast. A fused performance will depend in large part on the congruence of symbols and meanings, performed and interpreted, on both textual and performative levels of representation.

Actors

In theater and in social life, actors are the people who encode the meanings and put patterned representations of the script into practice, which demands competence in the requisite skills. In the case of musical performers, actors are the creators of music, the composers and musicians.[3] The requisite skills, at the most basic level, are knowledge of compositional craft and instrumental or vocal technique. Other skills required are a matter of historical variation. For example, extensive knowledge of court etiquette, especially ballet dancing, was required of musicians in J. S. Bach's time (see Little and Jenne 2001). At the end of the twentieth century, acting skills began to be demanded of opera singers. In the realm of popular "top 40" music, dancing ability has become increasingly important over the last two decades. The musical actor's aim is to use the mastery of these skills to obscure the constructedness of a performance. They aim for there to be no distinction between their performance and the background symbols they are invoking. In other words, they want the audience to believe they are *fused* with the meanings of the text, directly embodying them through performance.

This fusion of performer and meanings is less problematic when composers perform their own compositions. When the role of the composer and performer are combined in one person, the constructedness of the performance is reduced, and the ambiguous and open-ended quality of the performance ritual is attenuated. This explains the power of the composer/performer phenomenon since the rise of the work-concept ideology in the nineteenth century (see Goehr 1992). Bach, Mozart, Beethoven, Liszt, and Chopin are merely some of the most famous examples in music history, but they were hardly unusual in their day. The composer/performer phenomenon is assumed more authentic in other musical traditions as well, as demonstrated in the privileged position of the singer/songwriter in folk music and the lower status of cover bands in rock music.[4] What deserves sociological attention is the social construction of the musical actor when the roles of composer and performer are not merged into one person. To an important extent, this separation of roles poses a problem of performance to be overcome.

The Audience and Other Observers

Like all modes of cultural performance, musical performance is a social process in which meaning is displayed for others. Therefore, it requires an audience. Stravinsky (2003 [1942]) once wrote in a rare moment of romanticism, "A work of art cannot contain itself. Once he has completed his work, the creator necessarily feels the need to share his joy. He quite naturally seeks to establish contact with his fellow man, who in this case becomes his listener. The listener reacts and becomes a partner in the game, initiated by the creator" (131). For Benjamin Britten, the audience completes the "holy triangle" of the musical experience, which "needs three human beings at least. It requires a composer, a performer, and a listener; and unless these three take part together, there is no musical experience" (quoted in Simms 1999:180).

The audience can be present (e.g., in the concert hall) or imagined (e.g., in the practice room). Thanks to recording technology, the intended audience need not even be present at the moment of performance. In every case, the role of the audience is critical; they have the power to reject, subvert, or transform the meanings of the musical performance. But more important for our purposes, the audience in contemporary societies tends to be both fragmented and stratified, which means that different segments of the audience decode musical performance in various and often unpredictable ways. For instance, one could find among the audience members of a symphony concert any of the following: critics, professional musicians, friends and family of the composer or performer(s), subscription ticket holders, music students, symphony patrons, ushers and other concert hall staff, and (hopefully) a few novices to classical music. Because they are differently positioned, differently equipped, and differently invested in the musical performance, segments of the audience draw on different background symbols for their interpretation. These interpretations can be more or less congruent with each other, and it depends on the context of performance whether incongruence will disrupt the ritual and interfere with the social performance. Needless to say, performance has the highest chance of fusion when actors and audience are drawing on the same system of collective representations and agree on the style in which these should be performed.

The degree of audience fragmentation varies depending on performance context and musical genre. This is a matter of empirical investigation. But the problem of audience cohesion is a challenge for both performer and composer. The musical actor must decide whether she will design a multilayered performance that might be meaningful in different ways to different audiences, or instead direct her performance to a primary audience of "significant others." Milton Babbitt (1999 [1958]) articulated the latter option in its extreme in his controversial article "Who Cares If You Listen? (The Composer as Specialist)." In his view, "contemporary serious music" had truly diverged from "traditional music," reaching a level that demanded highly specialized knowledge. The general public who lacked this knowledge were likely to be bored or frustrated by contemporary music, provoking them to dismiss it as decadent and blame the composer for his isolation. Rather than compromise his or her work and cater to the general public, Babbitt believed it would be more appropriate for the composer to restrict performances of new compositions to an audience of specialists in the university. In his view, advanced music should be no different from other highly specialized fields, like mathematics and science. For this reason, he boldly suggested that

> the composer would do himself and his music an immediate and eventual service by total, resolute, and voluntary withdrawal from this public world to one of private performance and electronic media, with its very real possibility of complete elimination of the public and social aspects of musical composition. By so doing the separation between the domains would be defined beyond any possibility of confusion of categories, and the composer would be free to pursue a private life of professional achievement, as opposed to a public life of unprofessional compromise and exhibitionism. (quoted in Simms 1999:158)

This suggestion was vehemently rejected by many of Babbitt's peers, especially his European colleagues, who believed it was the composer's duty to be socially relevant. To be fair to Babbitt, however, he was not calling for a blanket retreat of new music to the ivory tower, only composers of the kind of "serious music" he had defined very precisely—total serialism. He hoped to find a protected environment in which this completely rationalized method of composition could evolve into a system of collective representations.

The audience's attention, and the primary system of collective representations they invoke in interpretation, are among the most important conditions of performance that composers have sought to control, or at least anticipate. This is why recording technology posed such a threat to classical music composers when it was first introduced. For Britten, the loudspeaker in particular was the "principal enemy of music" because it removed all responsibility from the listener and made the performance of music possible in any venue, regardless of its suitability for the piece in question. While this technology might aid education and study, it was a "deluding" substitute for true musical experience. As he explained:

> Music demands more from a listener than simply the possession of a tape machine or a transistor radio. It demands some preparation, some effort—a journey to a special place, saving up for a ticket, some homework on the program perhaps, some clarification of the ears and sharpening of the instincts. It demands as much effort on the listener's part as the other two corners of the triangle, this holy triangle of composer, performer, and listener. (quoted in Simms 1999:180)

Adorno and Stravinsky similarly condemned the radio. They believed that if music were too easily available and required no effort other than turning the dial, listening practices would deteriorate into habit. Music would no longer serve as a bearer of social truth, but would become like a drug, stultifying rather than stimulating the critical sensibilities of the mind.

While these arguments have usually been dismissed as nostalgia or conservative ranting, we might do better to use them as insight into a problem of performance. Composers write pieces for certain occasions with specific venues in mind knowing that these help determine the collective representations the audience will use in their interpretations. For example, Bach's Passions were written for performance in a Lutheran church on Good Friday. To remove these works from their intended sacred venue for performance on a concert stage is to distance them from the primary system of collective representations—Lutheran Christianity—that was meant to guide their interpretation. For this reason, many composers have disapproved of this practice. But recording technologies went even further; they were not only taking works into different concert venues than those intended but promising to free music from the performance ritual altogether. Any music could potentially be heard anywhere, and it no longer needed to be the focus of the listener's attention. To the composer, this technology represented a considerable loss of control over the conditions of performance and therefore a potential distortion of the intended meanings encoded in the score.

Here I have addressed the audience from the point of view of the musical actor, specifically the composer, and how the anticipated audience influences the process of encoding meanings into musical scripts. In future work, I plan to investigate this question from the point of view of the performer, examining how anticipated audience reaction guides not only one's choice of scripts (repertoire) but also the enactment of these meanings (performance practice or style) in different performance situations. But the analysis would remain incomplete if it neglected to address the social processes through which audiences interpret the meanings displayed by musical actors. It is here that the performance perspective can incorporate insights and methods from the field of reception studies. Although the best of this work has concentrated on recorded music, it has also explored performance contexts where the audience consists of a single individual (DeNora 2003; Bull 2000) as well as social groups (DeNora 1995). I agree with Hennion (2001) that the most promising way to understand the act of listening is to see it as a performance, but this topic cannot be pursued here.

The Means of Symbolic Production

In order to perform the script in hand in front of an audience, the performer requires access to a range of material things. In musical performance, these things range from clothing to wear, to instruments to play, to the venue for a performance. These material things are neither mundane nor insignificant. They can either provide the performer with a wealth of devices to enable nuanced symbolic projections, or they can undermine meanings and subvert the performer's intentions.

Consider, for example, the concert hall. Ideally, this is not only a venue dedicated to the music performance ritual but also an amplification device, making the most subtle performative nuance perceptible even to the audience member furthest from the stage. Although we tend to take these places for granted, it was not until the late eighteenth century that buildings designed specifically for the purpose of musical performances were constructed. Previously, music had been "functional," written for specific political or religious rituals and performed in spaces constructed for these purposes. It was not set apart from, but participated in, other realms of social life. The purpose-built concert hall is the result of a number of significant social and cultural changes, including the rise of the bourgeois public, the idea of a "functionless" music, the eclipsing of vocal music by abstract instrumental music, and the establishment of music as an autonomous art form worthy of aesthetic criticism.

Elsewhere I have argued that the architecture of the symphony concert hall both reflects and directs the ritual practice of the public concert (McCormick 2003). Architecture is neither neutral nor innocent; the organization of space created through the built environment reflects cultural understandings and beliefs about social practices, such as music making. While architecture might not absolutely dictate how inhabitants use space, it does suggest certain uses by creating conditions conducive to some activities and not others. In this sense, a building is a social performance. Through the arrangement of physical materials into forms, architects display meanings to a varied audience (including clients, peers, critics, etc.) who interpret these meanings by invoking various symbolic frameworks. And, like the audience of musical scripts who can identify with the meanings displayed or subvert them, inhabitants of buildings can cooperate or resist the meanings displayed by the built environment.

The meanings encoded in the ideal-typical concert hall invite a Durkheimian interpretation. No matter whether it is built in North America, Europe, or Asia, the concert hall is usually set apart from other buildings, surrounded by a plaza, and symbolically elevated on a hill. Upon entering the front of the building, the audience member does not enter the performance space directly but passes first through a lobby area. Passageways direct the public's journey toward the room at the heart of the building where the music is performed. In this way, the audience is taken through a liminal passage before entering the ritual space. Performers similarly pass through the liminal backstage area where they prepare for their performance. The performance space itself is designed to set the music apart from mundane social life, removing as many potential visual and aural distractions as possible. The seats are arranged to restrict movement, discourage conversation, and direct the public's gaze to the stage. Daylight is usually blocked out in order for controlled artificial lighting to signal when and where attention should be focused. Sound locks seal out external noise and potential disruptions, such as traffic, rain, or passers-by. Much to the dismay of musicians, the architect can do nothing for the aural distractions within the hall. The materials used in the performance space are carefully chosen for their acoustic properties, but they do not discriminate. A flattering acoustic will amplify coughs and candy wrappers as much as it will carry the most delicate *pianissimo* passage.

Traditionally, the arrangement of space in this room placed performers and audiences across from each other. Whether in a "shoe-box" or "shell" shape, this has been the preferred design for acoustic reasons. But the opposition of performers and audience also suggests a relationship between them, and recently this physical arrangement has been interpreted as an expression of the audience's alienation (see Small 1998). The grand formality of the concert hall that was once interpreted as solemn or inspiring is instead interpreted as stodgy or intimidating. For this reason, architects have been experimenting with the design of the concert hall to create a more intimate experience. The first successful departure from the shoe-box design was Hans Scharoun's highly acclaimed Philharmonic Hall in Berlin (completed in 1963.) This hall features a "vineyard design" of terraced balconies that encircle the stage. Frank Gehry also succeeded in designing a concert space in the round without sacrificing acoustics in the Walt Disney Concert Hall in Los Angeles (completed in 2003). By altering the physical relationship between performers and audience in the music room, these architects hope to suggest new interpretations of the concert experience. In Gehry's case, he was striving to build a democratic music room that could hold more than two thousand people and still feel intimate (personal communication, Frank Gehry, April 29, 2004). The popularity of his building with critics, musicians, and audience members alike suggests that the space for musical performance also carries meaning, and that this too is subject to historical and cultural variation.

Unusual venues can also suggest new interpretations of musical texts. For example, cellist Matt Heimovitz has recently been performing classical repertoire on his 1710 Goffriler cello in clubs, bars, and even barns in addition to the world's great concert halls. He enjoys the distinction of being the first classical artist to play at CBGB, birthplace of American punk. New music ensembles have always been interested in performing in nontraditional venues to distance themselves symbolically from classical music and all its associations. For example, Bang on a Can has performed its famous Marathon concerts in spaces as diverse as art galleries, experimental theaters, and popular music venues. Similarly, Alarm Will Sound transformed the Roxy night club in Chelsea, Manhattan, into a salon setting for a Steve Reich retrospective recording session.

Other means of symbolic production are also at the disposal of the musical actor. Clothing, for example, offers the performer a repertoire of visual symbols. Although wardrobe might seem to have little to do with effective performance of the musical text, it plays an integral part of what Richard Leppert (1993) has called the "sight of sound." We are more likely to think this an issue for popular music, but it applies equally to the art music tradition. It is because of the symbolic power of wardrobe that orchestras have a strict dress code; their reluctance to discard the tuxedo is symbolic of their strong link to tradition. Classical musicians who are bold enough to experiment with their wardrobe are gambling with their largest audience.

Take, for example, Vanessa Mae, the first poster girl of classical music, who is remembered in classical music circles as much for her gauzy blouses as for her technique, or the reaction to Nigel Kennedy's decision to sport a mohawk hairstyle to play Vivaldi's Four Seasons. New music ensembles, of course, are more likely to sport leather trousers than tuxedos. Similar to their use of nontraditional venues, this is part of an effort to align themselves with other renegade and cutting-edge musics and intentionally distance themselves from the high-art tradition from which they are descended. Different fragments of the audience will interpret these symbolic elements differently. To some, they might come across as shallow gimmick or crass commercialism. To others, they will come across as innovative and appealing. The challenge for the performer is to integrate visual symbols with other meanings performed and be as convincing in this aspect of performance as he or she is in others.

In the last sixty years, recording technologies have introduced a new range of means and tools for the musical actor. Editing software enables musicians to adjust their performances until they match their ideal realization of a musical text. If the performer so wishes, the contingencies of performance—nerves, an ill-timed cough in the audience, a late entrance in the wind section, an imperfect tuning of the instrument—can be eliminated entirely. The possibility of a "perfect" recording was cited among the reasons why Canadian pianist Glenn Gould abandoned the concert stage in favor of the recording studio at the height of his career in 1964. The distribution of these recordings has also allowed the performer to reach an audience larger than the most extensive touring schedule. Neither should it be forgotten that new recording technologies brought with them new visual media to the music world, from the graphic design of album covers and liner notes to the music video.

For the classical musician, the most significant means of symbolic production is the musical instrument itself. The craft of instrument making is indeed an art in its own right that the technologies of mass production have never been able to match. The most famous luthiers—Stradivari, Amati, Guarneri, Tecchler, Montagnana, and Vuillaume, to name a few—earned their reputations by constructing instruments that combine the most desirable qualities: durability of construction, richness of tone, dynamic range, flexibility and variety in tone color, equal projection across registers, and maneuverability. The musical instrument is the means of symbolic production at the most fundamental level; a performer is much more likely to enact a good performance if he or she has an instrument that is highly responsive, easy to play, and capable of projecting the most delicate nuances to the back of the hall. All the audio technology in the world cannot compensate for a musical instrument of poor quality because the musical performance is the outcome of an interaction between performer and instrument; the capabilities of the instrument influence not only the sounds produced in action but also the imagination of the performer. Fine instruments bring new meaning to the phrase "playing an instrument," inspiring the performer to experiment and risk new sounds. Instruments are believed to have personalities that can work with or against that of the musician. This is why, despite the prohibitive cost, concert pianists prefer to tour with their own instrument rather than risk finding themselves incompatible with the local piano for an important performance.

Mise-en-Scène

"With texts and means in hand, and audience(s) before them, social actors engage in dramatic social action, entering into and projecting the ensemble of physical and verbal gestures that constitute performance"(Alexander 2004:532). Bringing the text "to life," the process of actualizing textual interpretation, is not as straightforward a matter as it might seem. Musicians know this as the issue of *style* or, in scholarly circles dealing with ancient music, performance practice. The contingency and variability of the mise-en-scène proves that the text/script/score is neither self-evident nor complete.[5]

    Mise-en-scène refers to musicians' ability, or failure, to understand how to perform a text in a way that is meaningful to the audience. This involves not only musicians' ability to interpret the score—to understand the gesture, effect, or phrase in question and how it relates to the work's formal structure—but also the ability to actualize their interpretations and communicate them effectively to an audience in a contingent performance situation. In the eighteenth century, this was described as a matter of *bon goût,* or taste; now we are more likely to describe this as knowing the "right way" to play the piece in question. Technical mastery is necessary but not sufficient and, in some cases, beside the point. Musical performance is not like typing, where it is simply a matter of playing the right notes in the right order and at the right time. This is the problem with speaking of performance as the final stage of production. Performance is not supplementary, but constitutive, of the product that occasions it.

Style is the result of a complex interaction between audience expectation and performance techniques constrained by the possibilities of the text. A musician wanting to perform a piece in a meaningful way to a given audience will have at her disposal a range of expressive tools that she will employ to achieve that effect. Her stylistic repertoire, and the degree of her freedom to experiment, is largely determined by the musical genre. Should the performer's experiments with style venture too far into unfamiliar territory, she might render the text uninterpretable or meaningless to the audience. Depending on the performer's reputation and the manner of presentation, an experimental performance can invite accusations of incompetence, insanity, irreverence, or "selling out."

Style is also subject to historical variation. It would be unfair, however, to explain this away as a changing of "fashion" or a gradual acceptance of deviance because stylistic change is interwoven with transformations in compositional style and instrument construction. The most famous example is the use of *vibrato* (a regular fluctuation of pitch and or intensity, coming from the Latin for "to shake"). This technical device has been used in Western music as far back as the Middle Ages. In the baroque period, vibrato was considered an ornament used occasionally to convey "a meaning in accord with Baroque conceptions of passions or with a character as portrayed in a given piece of music." To overuse this effect was in poor taste; it was used only "sparingly, for emphasis on long, accentuated notes in pieces with an affect or character to which it was suited." Used indiscriminately, it would lose its association with "fear, cold, death, sleep and mourning" or its connotation with feminine sweetness (Moens-Haenen, n.d.).

Over the course of the nineteenth century, more performers were using vibrato continuously to embellish tone, much to the dismay of many teachers and theorists. This was hardly an indulgence on the part of performers. The eighteenth-century obsession with resonance had been replaced with an interest in sustained tone which was considered desirable for compositions in the new romantic style. Performers also had to worry about projection in concert halls of ever-increasing size. To this end, string instruments were being redesigned, from the introduction of metal strings to replace gut, to the lengthened neck to increase string tension, to the new Tourte bow design with a larger tip and a convex, rather than concave, stick shape. These changes in compositional style and instrument construction called for new performance techniques, such as the increased use of vibrato. By the twentieth century, the baroque connotations were long forgotten, and vibrato became so common that it was its absence (*senza vibrato*) that created the dramatic effect. As it was no longer considered a sign of poor technique or questionable taste, string players were being trained to use vibrato continuously on every note, coloring their tone through alterations of speed and width.

This is only one example of research into historical performance practice that preoccupied the classical music world for at least twenty years. Questions of intonation, temperament, instrument construction, tempo, instrumentation, bowings, fingerings, articulation, and ornamentation have been painstakingly researched and debated because ours is the first time in history that musicians have had to research performance practices of earlier historical periods in order to perform historical scores in a meaningful way to their audience. This is no simple matter; the musician must now also be a scholar rummaging through archives and interpreting historical documents that are usually contradictory and raise more questions than they answer.

It was not always so. When Felix Mendelssohn conducted a performance of Bach's *St. Matthew Passion* at the Sing-Akademie in 1829, he made his own arrangement of the score. Cuts, changes, and additions were made in order to perform this historical work in a meaningful way to the audience of his day. Mendelssohn obviously knew what he was doing, because the performance was a great success and proved to be the turning point in Bach's revival. Hegel, who was present at this performance, later wrote of "Bach's grand, truly Protestant, robust and erudite genius which we have only recently learnt again to appreciate at its full value" (Temperly and Wollny, n.d.).

Today's audiences are unlikely to tolerate such liberties with the score, and few conductors would dare to try. Of course, not all musicians have embraced the performance practice movement with equal fervor and still enjoy great careers. Rostropovich's most recent recordings of Bach are still performed in a romantic style. But others, including the Eroica quartet, are expanding performance practice scholarship to music of the nineteenth century. The authenticity movement has definitely made its mark in the music world, and thanks to recording technology, we can trace this change.[6] Audiences today, especially in Europe, have become so accustomed to historical performance practice that they are likely to protest performances that would have been applauded enthusiastically a few decades ago. Few conductors would dare to stage Handel's Messiah with two full-size orchestras and four choirs, an artistic decision that made perfect sense in the 1950s.

Although it might seem that these matters are only of concern to highly trained specialists, the performance practice debate is of considerable sociological significance. Taruskin (1995) has persuasively demonstrated that the authenticity debate is quintessentially modern, a product of the aesthetic and cultural values of our time. He contrasts two performing sensibilities, the "vitalist" and "authentistic" point of view. While the former construes intention internally, guided by spiritual, emotional, or metaphysical matters, the latter is firmly rooted in positivism. Operating on the basis of objectivity and authority rather than identification and subjectivity, the "authentistic" approach to performance seeks to derive normative procedures from empirically ascertainable facts to determine how texts should be realized. This is particularly evident in the kind of language adopted by one of the authenticity movement's most famous proponents, Christopher Hogwood, "who looks forward to the day when we will be able, after digesting "sufficient data," to make "rules and regulations" to govern performances of nineteenth-century music" (Taruskin 1995:97). In its more radical forms, the "authentistic" point of view betrays the dehumanizing tendencies of modernity. Here, Taruskin deserves to be quoted at length:

> Ever since we have had a concept of "classical" music we have implicitly regarded our musical institutions as museums and our performers as curators. Curators do not own the artifacts in their charge. [...] And hence the magical aura that has attached in the minds of many, to "original instruments"; for they are artifacts as concretely, tangibly, and objectively authentic as an Old Master painting, and those who use them can claim ipso facto to be better curators than those who do not. But though the instruments are objects, the pieces they play are not. And hence the falseness, nay the evil, of the notion so widespread at the moment, that the activity of our authentistic performer is tantamount to that of a restorer of paintings, who strip away the accumulated dust and grime of centuries to lay bare an original object in all its pristine splendor. In musical performance, neither what is removed nor what remains can be said to possess an objective ontological existence akin to that of dust or picture. Both what is "stripped" and what is "bared" are *acts* and both are interpretations—unless you can conceive of a performance, say, that has no tempo, or one that has no volume or tone color. [...] But that is not the worst of it. What is thought of as the "dirt" when musicians speak of restoring

a piece of music is what people, acting out of an infinite variety of motives over the years, have done with it. What is thought of as the "painting" by such musicians is an imaginary rendering in which "personal choices" have been "reduced to a minimum," and, ideally, eliminated. What this syllogism reduces to is: *people are dirt.* (149–50, emphasis in original)

Distinguishable from performance practice issues, but also of central importance to the mise-en-scène, are what I would like to call "performance traditions." These are the stylistic details that have less to do with carefully researched techniques and more to do with inheritance passed on from teacher to pupil in performing communities. Performance traditions are sometimes the product of historical accident. For example, a number of chamber music works are still performed with dramatic pauses that had their origin in the awkward page turns of editions long out of print. But it is more often the case that performance traditions are consciously enacted in order to invoke one's "instrumental inheritance." Performers often imitate their teacher's manner of walking on stage and posture at the instrument, as well as consciously adopt their teachers' practical solutions to "problems" of performance. For example, some cellists have placed their chair beside, rather than in front of the piano for recital performances.

There is a practical component to these acts—the placement of the cellist beside the piano addresses some balance problems in certain repertoire. But they are also symbolic. Through these acts, performers are displaying their lineage and, consequently, the performance philosophies that guided their training. A cellist sitting beside the piano can also be interpreted as a departure from the "soloistic" approach to the performance of sonatas, and symbolic of a "partnership" approach to music making and performing. Conservatories, based on the guild system, are inherently conservative and make the various instrumental traditions (German, Russian, French) easy to trace. Often these practices are of more significance to fellow instrumentalists; few audience members would care too much about the length of the cellist's end pin or bowing technique. But some performance traditions become strongly associated with the great icons of performance and thereby become intensely meaningful both to the performers who reenact them and to the audience members who recognize them. For example, the opening of the Elgar Cello Concerto has become almost unimaginable without Jacqueline du Pré's famous slide.

Performance practice and performance traditions refer to those aspects of the mise-en-scène that are within the control of the performer. But the performer's greatest challenge is learning how to adapt these techniques spontaneously and effectively in a contingent performance situation. Some aspects of the mise-en-scène will always remain beyond the performer's control—an overly resonant performance space, a distracted audience, a string that gets knocked out of tune halfway through the piece, a series of unflattering reviews in the press. The skilled performer knows how to make these go unnoticed or turn them to their advantage.[7]

Social Power

The final element in the analysis of musical performance is social power. This refers to "the distribution of power in society—the nature of its political, economic, and status hierarchies, and the relations among its elites" and how it affects the process of social performance (Alexander 2004:532). The effects of unequal power distribution apply to every element of performance discussed earlier, and it is here that we can apply the insights of the production perspective and Pierre Bourdieu.

Many systems of collective representations can apply to a musical performance, but some are deemed more legitimate than others. One's access to, and facility with, the most privileged system of meaning is part of how status is achieved and sustained, as Bourdieu (1984) showed with meticulous empirical precision in *Distinction*. At the level of the actor, social power is manifested in the form of reputation. When one has developed a reputation, in the sense of receiving positive recognition, it can function as a form of symbolic capital:

> For the author, the critic, the art dealer, the publisher or the theatre manager, the only legitimate accumulation consists in making a name for oneself, a known, recognized name, a capital of consecration implying a power to consecrate objects (with a trademark or signature) or persons (through publication, exhibition, etc.) and therefore to give value, and to appropriate the profits from this operation. (Bourdieu 1993c:75)

Although Bourdieu directed this observation to the fields of literature, visual art, and theater, it can easily be extended to musical performance. Reputation allows some musical actors to be indulged or even applauded for their risky performance experiments, while others are quickly dismissed as charlatans. Like any other form of power, it can be converted into other forms of capital. It can be used to acquire better means of symbolic production, like expensive instruments or a recording label, or to gain access to highly visible social or musical platforms, like televised concerts and personal introductions to elites in other fields. In this way, symbolic capital can be invested inside one's own field of production or used as currency in another social realm. For example, cellist Mstislav Rostropovich used his charisma and his resources to champion contemporary music, a marginalized music in his field of cultural production. His international fame and prestige also granted him access to the international press for his protest against the Soviet government's treatment of artists.

Reputation, however, is socially constructed by the audience, as DeNora (1995) has demonstrated in her work on Beethoven. To use Bourdieu's phrase, the sociologist must investigate who "creates the creator." Segments of the audience with more cultural capital are better positioned to invest the composer or performer with symbolic worth. Conversely, performers can be symbolically polluted if embraced by a less legitimate audience. Neither should the influence of critics be forgotten. They have their own means of symbolic production to broadcast their evaluation of the musical performance to the wider audience; their expertise and resources position them well to support or subvert the interpretation of the performer's intended meanings.

Sociological analysis must also account for the patterns of inequality that structure the social world in which music is performed. To begin, it should explain the social sources of restrictions and barriers placed on participation in musical performance. In Western art music, musical roles continue to be gendered, and access to training continues to be restricted by class. Access to the means of symbolic production is also stratified. For example, not everyone can afford good musical instruments. Because their value is determined in part by the collector's market, string instruments are often priced beyond the performer's means. It is for this reason that governments and universities have started purchasing fine instruments to loan to promising performers. Government subsidy is one example of how political power can support musical performance through the provision of material resources and legitimacy. But political power can also restrict musical performance through the censorship of musical texts or the restriction of the resources necessary to realize their performance. Even when the means of symbolic production are obtained by performers, it does not guarantee the presence or attention of an audience. Venues for presenting performances are themselves stratified. Those that could endow a performance with their symbolic weight or help establish the reputation of an up-and-coming artist are often the territory of economic and artistic elites who erect organizational systems of gatekeeping to protect their prestige.

The guiding purpose of studies in the production perspective, and their great contribution, has been to demonstrate that the structure of the field of production and broader social inequality must not be bracketed because they profoundly influence the creation, performance, and interpretation of the musical text. By structuring the social context in which musical performances occur, social power explains why some performers are more likely than others to find a felicitous environment for the enactment and interpretation of musical/social meaning.

CONCLUSION

The problem with the production/consumption paradigm, especially in its most recent incarnation, is that it has intentionally reduced explanation to the element of social power alone. Although the analyst must account for the dynamics of social power and their effects on musical performance, an analysis that is restricted to this element will always be partial and misleading. If one chooses to be blind to the social relevance of the other elements of performance, social power is easily mistaken for the ultimate determinant of the meaning of musical/social performances. The most obvious guilty party in this respect has been the production perspective. Less concerned with the intended meaning of cultural products, it has deliberately focussed on "how the content of culture is influenced by the milieux in which it is created, distributed, evaluated, taught, and preserved," seeking methods that "facilitate the uncovering of the so-called 'unintended' consequences of purposive productive activity" (Peterson 1994:164–65). To this end, it has typically borrowed from the sociology of organizations, industry, and occupations in order to compare similar structural processes in realms of cultural production as diverse as art, science, and religion. To make this sort of broad comparison, cultural products are necessarily secondary to the social processes of interest. In its more benign form, this kind of analysis exhibits an agnostic attitude toward the cultural object. But the "uncovering unintended consequences" can also evolve into a project of demystification.

This has certainly been the case with the art worlds approach. In Howard Becker's (1982) case, he confesses that a "congenital anti-elitism" motivated his analytical perspective (ix). This helps explain why his contribution to the sociology of art is not as a symbolic interactionist but as a sociologist of work. Becker is himself a performing jazz musician, so it is not surprising that his concept of "convention" resonates with much of what I have discussed in this chapter. But

Becker's antielitism forces him to deny art as symbolic action; and to demystify it, he must disenchant it. In his analysis, conventions are not symbolic structures that guide the communication and interpretation of meaning, but time and labor saving devices in cultural production. For example, it is convention that dictates the division of labor between composer and performer and other "support personnel." It is convention that coordinates the work involved in producing a concert. It is also convention that guides the materials that constitute the musical text (e.g., the diatonic scale) as well as the performance style that suits audience taste. Convention is not so rigid that change is impossible; innovation is regularly introduced through deviance. (His example is vibrato in string playing, which is why I have discussed it at length.) While one can depart from convention, it comes at a cost. Unconventional work is not only more difficult to accomplish; it is also likely to meet resistance from others because it can undermine the stability of the art world's organizational structure.

The major weakness of Becker's concept is that it is called on to cover too much ground. It simply includes too vast a terrain of practices. How can the diatonic scale be a convention in the same way and on the same level as the rituals of concert hall etiquette or the dress of the orchestra? And these examples are all drawn from the same musical genre. Becker fails to offer the analytical tools necessary to identify how different kinds of conventions function in different artistic disciplines in different historical circumstances. A performance perspective provides the analytical categories necessary to refine this concept. Each element of performance distinguishes conventions of a different order and kind. For example, the conventions that organize the form of the musical text are contained in the category of *script*. The *mise-en-scène* includes conventions that structure the realization of these texts. With "performance practice" and "performance traditions," I have tried to distinguish two kinds of conventions within the broader analytical category. No doubt more would emerge through empirical investigation of a particular genre of musical performance. But most important, a performance perspective recognizes conventions as inherently cultural. Conventions accomplish more than the efficient coordination of artistic labor; they are the very mechanisms of rituals. Conventions can order interaction only to the extent that everyone understands and identifies with their purpose and content. Departure from convention is threatening to the stability of an art world not because it has become habit but because it signifies the breaking of a social contract, a divergence from the form and content of interaction that had become heavily invested with meaning. It undermines the shared understandings upon which cultural performance is based.

The trap of the production perspective and the art world approach is that they not only bracket meaning but systematically deny it on three distinct levels. The first is that of the artwork. Having taken the position that meaning cannot be inscribed in the artwork, the only possible source of meaning is its social use. Aura is thereby eclipsed and the artwork is "revealed" to be merely a mundane object. The second level is the aesthetic action of the artist. Having identified social processes and not individuals as the major causal force in artistic worlds (Peterson 1994), talent or creativity is effectively denied. "Artist" is therefore an arbitrary title attached to an occupation that participates in a complex division of labor guided by conventions. Logically, then, esteem is not enjoyed due to the demonstration of unique ability; it is only bestowed if it can benefit powerful groups in that social world. Artistic genius is therefore "unmasked" as groundless (but calculated) belief. The third level involves the aesthetic action of the art world. If artworks are not inherently meaningful, there is no reason to engage with them unless they can help accomplish certain ends. Art audiences, then, are not interpreting meaningful objects but consuming strategically either to create or maintain a social boundary. Patrons of the arts are therefore not performing a public service or participating in a meaningful activity but using art as a resource in status accumulation (DiMaggio 1982). Any claim to the contrary is dismissed as smoke screen or self-delusion. Having denied *Wertrational,* aesthetic appreciation is "exposed" as instrumental action.

To be fair, the bracketing of meaning has been less pronounced on the consumption side of the production/consumption paradigm. Some reception studies have endeavored to examine the social processes through which artworks become meaningful. Often adopting an ethnomethedological approach, these studies examine concrete acts of engagement where individuals use art objects, such as music, as a resource in various forms of action such as identity formation, experience of public space, or the channeling of emotion (see De-Nora 2003; Bull 2000). The strength of this perspective is that it expands music's social significance from that of a status weapon. It offers insight into the experience of music through sensitive analyses of situated engagement with aesthetic objects. But it also inherits the methodological individualism of ethnomethodology, restricting interpretive frameworks to the concrete circumstances of the specific event. There is meaning, but it remains the private project of the individual and the product of a specific, self-contained occasion. Through the concept of mise-en-scène, the performance perspective can preserve the attention to contingency while the system of collective representations can address how broader cultural codes inform the structure of that occasion and the interpretive frameworks brought into play. The performance perspective can also transcend the problematic production/consumption dichotomy that artificially restricts meaning making to the moment of reception.

It is the exclusive attention to social power and the structure of fields of production that has earned sociology the reputation of offering a narrow and cynical view of aesthetic practice, but it is the production/consumption paradigm that has prevented our discipline from understanding music as a performing art. Through this brief outline of the performance perspective, I hope to have shown that the production of culture and art worlds perspectives need not be entirely refuted but instead incorporated into a multidimensional theoretical approach that brings the element of social power into proper relation with other aspects of musical performance. Sociology—especially the sociology of the arts—need not be a destructive or reductive discipline (Elias 1993 [1991]). It is not only possible but necessary to bring meaning back into the sociology of music without relapsing into naive romanticism.

NOTES

1. Some evidence of Carnegie Hall's status as sacred place: the saying associated with the hall, and printed on all its promotional merchandise, claims that "you haven't made it if you haven't played it." It is also a featured in a standard music joke: How do you get to Carnegie Hall? Practice!

2. Made famous by the Ramones, CBGB is known as the birthplace of American punk. See www.cbgb.com for a history of this New York City nightclub by its owner and founder, Hilly Kristal.

3. Stravinsky, of course, would not have considered the performer a creator of music as I have here. In his analysis, music has a peculiar nature in that it is characterized by two moments, or states—potential and actual music—that presuppose two kinds of musicians—the creator and the performer.

4. *Cover bands* are professional musical groups that perform songs made famous by other performers. The term *cover* comes from the early popular music industry and refers to a recording of a song made by performers other than those responsible for the original recording. A cover is not necessarily an exact copy but is always a recognizable version of a popular song. (See Robert Witmer and Anthony Marks's entry on the term in *Grove Music Online*.) The most extreme form of a cover band is the "tribute band" that imitates as closely as possible not only the music but also the fashion and style of the original performers.

5. Notated scores can only convey a skeletal outline of the composer's intentions for performance. That topic deserves a separate discussion that

will be pursued elsewhere. Here I am using *style* to refer to the manner of enacting what *is* included in the score. For example, a Vivaldi sonata can be played in the baroque or romantic style. In both cases, the performer would have played the same notes, but the music will sound very different even to an untrained ear. In popular music, different styles are thought of as "versions" of the same song. For example, Shania Twain frequently releases pop and country versions of her albums. Recognizable styles of performance relate directly to the concept of "musical vernacular" introduced earlier.

6. Indeed, when debates over historical performance practice first emerged, some argued that the authenticity movement was actually a plot construed by the recording companies. If it was discovered that the great masterworks had been performed "incorrectly," everyone would have to buy new "authoritative" versions for their collection.

7. An excellent example of turning mise-en-scène contingencies to the performer's advantage is a famous story told to all aspiring string players about the nineteenth-century violin virtuoso, Nicolo Paganini. When one of his strings broke in the middle of a performance, he did not excuse himself and go backstage to replace it. Instead, he finished the piece on the three remaining strings, dazzling his audience with the extraordinary technical ability this feat requires.

Bibliography

Adorno, Theodor W. 1978. "On the Social Situation of Music." *Telos* 35: 129–65.

———. 1984. *Aesthetic Theory.* Ed. Gretel Adorno and Rolf Tiedeman; trans. C. Lenhardt. London: Routledge and Kegan Paul.

———. 1992. *Notes to Literature.* New York: Columbia University Press.

———. 1993. "Commitment." In *The Essential Frankfurt School Reader,* ed. Andrew Adorno and Eike Gebhardt. New York: Continuum.

———. 1997. *Aesthetic Theory.* Ed. Gretel Adorno and Rolf Tiedemann; trans. and ed. Robert Hullot-Kentor. Minneapolis: University of Minnesota Press.

———. 2002. *Essays on Music.* Berkeley: University of California Press.

Alexander, Jeffrey C. 1989. "Rethinking Durkheim's Intellectual Development: On the Complex Origins of a Cultural Sociology." In *Structure and Meaning: Relinking Classical Sociology.* New York: Columbia University Press.

———. 1995. "The Reality of Reduction: The Failed Synthesis of Pierre Bourdieu." In *Fin de Siècle Social Theory: Relativism, Reduction, and the Problem of Reason.* New York: Verso.

———. 2003. *The Meaning of Social Life: A Cultural Sociology.* London: Oxford University Press.

———. 2004. "Cultural Pragmatics: Social Performance between Ritual and Strategy." *Sociological Theory* 22, no. 4: 527–73.

Alexander, Jeffrey C., Bernhard Giesen, and Jason Mast. 2006. *Social Performance: Symbolic Action, Cultural Pragmatics and Ritual.* Cambridge: Cambridge University Press.

Alexander, Jeffrey C., and Steve Sherwood. 2002. "Mythic Gestures: Robert Bellah and Cultural Sociology." In *Modernity and Meaning: A Festschrift for Robert Bellah,* ed. Richard Madsen et al. Berkeley: University of California Press.

Alexander, Jeffrey C., and Philip Smith, eds. 2005. *The Cambridge Companion to Durkheim.* New York: Cambridge University Press.

Alexander, Jeffrey C., Philip Smith, and Steve Sherwood. 1993. "Risking Enchantment: Theory and Method in Cultural Studies." *Culture: A Newsletter of the American Sociological Association* 8, no. 1: 10–14.

Andrews, Julia. 1994. *Painters and Politics in the People's Republic of China, 1949–1979.* Berkeley: University of California Press.

Andrews, Julia, and Gao Minglu. 1995. "The Avent-Garde's Challenge to Official Art." In *Urban Spaces in Contemporary China: The Potential for Autonomy and Community in Post-Mao China,* ed. Deborah S. Davis et al. Washington, D.C.: Woodrow Wilson Center Press.

Andrews, Julia, and Kuiyu Shen. 1998. *Century in Crisis: Modernity and Tradition in the Art of Twentieth-Century China.* New York: Guggenheim Museum.

Babbitt, Milton. 1999. "Who Cares If You Listen? (The Composer as Specialist)." In *Composers on Modern Musical Culture: An Anthology of Readings on Twentieth-Century Music,* ed. Bryan R. Simms. New York: Schirmer Books.

Barth, George. 1992. *The Pianist as Orator: Beethoven and the Transformation of Keyboard Style.* Ithaca, N.Y.: Cornell University Press.

Barthes, Roland. 1972. *Mythologies.* London: Cape.

———. 1993. *A Roland Barthes Reader.* London: Vintage.

Battersby, Christine. 1989. *Gender and Genius.* London: Woman's Press.

Baxandall, Michael. 1972. *Painting and Experience in Fifteenth-Century Italy.* London: Oxford University Press.

Becker, H. S. 1974. "Art as Collective Action." *American Sociological Review* 39: 767–76.

———. 1982. *Art Worlds.* Berkeley: University of California Press.

Becker, Howard, and Alain Pessin. Forthcoming. "A Dialogue on the Ideas of "World" and "Field."" *Opus 8*—Sociologie de l'art, nouvelle série.

Bellah, Robert. 1970. *Beyond Belief.* New York: Harper & Row.

Benjamin, Walter. 1968a. "Theses on the Philosophy of History." In *Benjamin: Illuminations,* ed. Hannah Arendt, trans. H. Zohh. New York: Harcourt, Brace & World.

———. 1968b. "The Work of Art in the Age of Mechanical Reproduction." In *Benjamin: Illuminations,* ed. Hannah Arendt, trans. H. Zohh. New York: Harcourt, Brace & World.

———. 1978. "The Author as Producer." In *Benjamin: Reflections,* ed. Peter Demetz, trans. E. Jephcott. New York: Harcourt Brace Jovanovich.

Berezin, Mabel. 1994. "Cultural Form and Political Meaning: State-Subsidized Theater, Ideology, and the Language of Style in Fascist Italy." *American Journal of Sociology* 99, no. 5: 1237–86.

Bernell, Robert, ed. 2002. *Chinese Artists, Texts and Interviews: Chinese Contemporary Art Awards (CCCA) 1998–2002.* Beijing: Timezone 8.

Bernstein, J. M. 1992. *The Fate of Art.* University Park: Pennsylvania State University Press.

Bian, Yanjie. 1994. *Work and Inequality in Urban China.* Albany: State University of New York Press.

Bourdieu, Pierre. 1984. *Distinction: A Social Critique of the Judgement of Taste.* Trans. R. Nice. Cambridge: Polity.

———. 1988. "The Invention of the Artist's Life." *Yale French Studies* 73: 75–103.

———. 1993a. *The Field of Cultural Production: Essays on Art and Literature.* Cambridge: Polity.

———. 1993b. "The Market of Symbolic Goods." In *The Field of Cultural Production: Essays on Art and Literature,* ed. R. Johnson. New York: Columbia University Press.

———. 1993c. "The Production of Belief: Contribution to an Economy of Symbolic Goods." In *The Field of Cultural Production: Essays on Art and Literature,* ed. R. Johnson. New York: Columbia University Press.

———. 1996. *The Rules of Art: Genesis and Structure of the Literary Field.* Cambridge: Polity.

Bourdieu, Pierre, A. Darbel, and D. Schnapper. 1997. *The Love of Art: European Art Museums and Their Public.* Cambridge: Polity.

Britten, Benjamin. 1999. "On Winning the First Aspen Award." In *Composers on Modern Musical Culture: An Anthology of Readings on Twentieth-Century Music,* ed. Bryan R. Simms. New York: Schirmer Books.

Bryson, Norman, et al., eds. 1994. Visual *Culture: Images and Interpretations.* Hanover, N.H.: Wesleyan University Press.

Bull, Michael. 2000. *Sounding Out the City: Personal Stereos and the Management of Everyday Life.* Oxford: Berg.

Burger, Peter. 1984. *Theory of the Avant-Garde.* Trans. M. Shaw. Minneapolis: University of Minnesota Press.

Burnham, Scott. 1995. *Beethoven Hero.* Princeton, N.J.: Princeton University Press.

———. 2000. "The Four Ages of Beethoven: Musicians (and a Few Others) on Beethoven." In *The Cambridge Companion to Beethoven,* ed. G. Stanley. Cambridge: Cambridge University Press.

Calhoun, Craig. 1994. "Civil Society and Public Sphere." In *Neither Gods nor Emperors: Students and the Struggle for Democracy in China.* Berkeley: University of California Press.

Calhoun, Craig, et al., eds. 1993. *Bourdieu: Critical Perspectives.* Chicago: University of Chicago Press.

Cameron, Catherine M. 1990. "Avant-Gardism as a Mode of Culture Change" *Cultural Anthropology* (May): 217–30.

Carroll, Noel. 1998. *A Philosophy of Mass Art.* New York: Oxford University Press.

Chipp, Herschel. 1968. *Theories of Modern Art: A Source Book by Artists and Critics.* Berkeley: University of California Press.

Citron, Marcia 1993. *Gender and the Musical Canon.* Cambridge: Cambridge University Press.

Clarke, E., and N. Cook. 2004. *Empirical Musicology: Aims, Methods, Prospects.* Oxford: Oxford University Press.

Clayton, M., T. Herbert, and R. Middleton, eds. 2003. *The Cultural Study of Music: A Critical Introduction.* London: Routledge.

Comini, Alessandra. 1987. *The Changing Image of Beethoven: A Study in Mythmaking.* New York: Rizzoli.

Cook, Nicholas. 2003. "Music as Performance." In *The Cultural Study of*

Music: A Critical Introduction, ed. Martin Clayton, Trevor Herbert, and Richard Middleton. New York: Routledge.

Crane, Diana. 1987. The *Transformation of the Avant-Garde: The New York Art World, 1940–1985*. Chicago: University of Chicago Press.

Danto, Arthur. 1997. *After The End of Art*. Princeton, N.J.: Princeton University Press.

Davies, Stephen. 1991. *Definitions of Art*. Ithaca, N.Y.: Cornell University Press.

Davis, Deborah. 2000. *The Consumer Revolution in Urban China*. Berkeley: University of California Press.

Dennis, David. 2000. "Beethoven at Large: Reception in Literature, the Arts, Philosophy and Politics." In *The Cambridge Companion to Beethoven*, ed. G. Stanley. Cambridge: Cambridge University Press.

DeNora, Tia. 1986. "How Is Extra-musical Meaning Possible? Music as a Place and Space for 'Work.'" *Sociological Theory* 84, no. 1: 84–94.

———. 1995. *Beethoven and the Construction of Genius: Musical Politics in Vienna, 1792–1803*. Berkeley: University of California Press.

———. 1996. "How Is Extra Musical Meaning Possible? Music as a Place and Space for 'Work.'" *Sociological Theory* 45: 84–94.

———. 1997. "The Biology Lessons of Opera Buffa." In *Opera Buffa in Mozart's Vienna*, ed. Mary Hunter and James Webster. Cambridge: Cambridge University Press.

———. 2000. *Music in Everyday Life*. Cambridge: Cambridge University Press.

———. 2002. "Music into Action: Performing Gender on the Viennese Concert Stage, 1790–1810." *Poetics* 30: 19–33.

———. 2003. *After Adorno: Rethinking Music Sociology*. Cambridge: Cambridge University Press.

———. 2004. "Embodiment and Opportunity: Bodily Capital, Gender and Reputation in Beethoven's Vienna." In *The Musician as Entrepreneur*, ed. W. Weber. Bloomington: Indiana University Press.

DiMaggio, Paul. 1982. "Cultural Entrepreneurship in Nineteenth-Century Boston: The Creation of an Organizational Base for High Culture in America." *Media, Culture and Society* 4: 33–50.

Downs, Philip. 1970. "Beethoven's 'New Way' and the Eroica." *Musical Quarterly* 56: 585–604.

Du Gay, Paul, et al. 1997. *Doing Cultural Studies: The Story of the Sony Walkman*. London: Sage.

Durkheim, Emile. 2001. *The Elementary Forms of the Religious Life*. Trans. C. Cosman. London: Oxford University Press.

Elias, Norbert. 1993. *Mozart: Portrait of a Genius*. Trans. Edmund Jephcott. Cambridge: Polity. Originally published as *Mozart: Zur Soziologie eines Genies* (Frankfurt am Main: Suhrkamp, 1991).

Ellis, Katherine. 1997. "Female Pianists and Their Male Critics in Nineteenth-Century Paris." *Journal of the American Musicological Society* 50: 353–85.

Eyerman, Ron. 1981. *False Consciousness and Ideology in Marxist Theory.* Atlantic Highlands, N.J.: Humanities Press.

———. 2002. *Cultural Trauma: Slavery and the Formation of African American Identity.* Cambridge: Cambridge University Press.

———. 2005. "The Murder of Theo van Gogh as Social Drama and Cultural Trauma." Yale Cultural Sociology Center Workshop, September 9. http://research.yale.edu/cs/workshop/0506/#week01a.

Eyerman, Ron, and Andrew Jamison. 1998. *Music and Social Movements: Mobilizing Traditions in the Twentieth Century.* Cambridge: Cambridge University Press.

Eyerman, Ronald, and Magnus Ring. 1998. "Towards a New Sociology of Art Worlds: Bringing Meaning Back In." *Acta Sociologica* 41, no. 3: 277–83.

Fields, Karen E. 1996. "Durkheim and the Idea of the Soul." *Theory and Society* 25, no. 2: 193–203.

Figes, Orlando. 2004. "The Truth about Shostakovich." *New York Review of Books* 51, no. 10, June 10, 2004.

Flack, Audrey. 1986. *Art and Soul: Notes on Creating.* New York: Dutton.

Fong, Wen C. 2001. *Between Two Cultures: Late Nineteenth and Twentieth-Century Chinese Paintings from the Robert H. Ellsworth Collection in the Metropolitan Museum of Art.* New York: Metropolitan Museum of Art.

Gadamer, Hans-Georg. 1987. *The Relevance of the Beautiful and Other Essays.* Cambridge: Cambridge University Press.

Gao Brothers (The). 2002. *The Chinese Avant-Garde Scene* [in Chinese]. Nanjing, Jiangsu: Jiangsu People's Press.

Gao, Minglu. 1991a. *The Century's Utopia: The Trends of Contemporary Chinese Avant-Garde Art.* Taipei: Artists Publishing House.

———. 1991b. *History of Modern Chinese Art 1985–1986* [in Chinese]. Shanghai: Shanghai People's Publishing House.

———. 1993. *Fragmented Memory: The Chinese Avant-Garde in Exile.* Columbus: Ohio State University.

———. 1998. *Inside Out: New Chinese Art.* San Francisco: San Francisco Museum of Modern Art; Asia Society Galleries; Berkeley: University of California Press.

Gao, Minglu, and Julia Andrews. 1995. "The Avant-Garde's Challenge to Official Art." In *Urban Spaces in Contemporary China,* ed. Deborah Davis et al. Cambridge: Cambridge University Press.

Gates, David, et al. "Lennon: The Battle over His Memory." *Newsweek,* October 17, 1988.

Gitlin, Todd. 1997. "The Anti-Political Populism of Cultural Studies." In *Cultural Studies in Question,* ed. Marjorie Ferguson and Peter Golding. London: Sage.

Goehr, Lydia. 1992. *The Imaginary Museum of Musical Works: An Essay in the Philosophy of Musical Works.* Oxford: Clarendon.

Goffman, Erving. 1972. *The Presentation of Self in Everyday Life.* New York: Knopf.

Grana, Cesar. 1989. *Meaning and Authenticity.* New Brunswick, N.J.: Transaction.

Greenberg, Clement. 1939. "Avant-Garde and Kitsch." In *Greenberg: The Collected Essays and Criticisms,* ed. John O' Brian. 4 vols. Chicago: University of Chicago Press.

Hall, Stuart. 1980. "Encoding/Decoding." In *Culture, Media, Language,* ed. Stuart Hall et al. London: Hutchinson.

Hall, Stuart, and Tony Jefferson. 1976. *Resistance through Rituals.* London: Hutchinson.

Halle, David.1993. *Inside Culture, Art and Class in the American Home.* Chicago: University of Chicago Press.

Harrington, Austin. 2004. *Art and Social Theory.* Cambridge: Polity.

Harrison, Charles. 1996. "Modernism." In *Critical Terms for Art History,* ed. Robert S. Nelson and R. Shiff. Chicago: University of Chicago Press.

Hay, Jonathan.2001. "Painting and the Built Environment in Late- Nineteenth-Century Shanghai." In *Chinese Art: Modern Expressions,* ed. M. Hearn and J. Smith. New York: Metropolitan Museum of Art.

Hennion, A. 2001. "Music Lovers: Taste as Performance." *Theory, Culture & Society* 18, no. 5: 1–22.

Herrero, Marta. 2005. *Irish Intellectuals and Aesthetics.* Dublin: Irish Academic Press.

Hood, Margaret. 1986. "Nannette Streicher and Her Pianos." *Continuo* (May): 2–5 and (June): 2–7.

Horkheimer, Max, and Theodor W. Adorno. 1986. *Dialectic of Enlightenment.* London: Verso.

———. 2002. *Dialectic of Enlightenment.* Stanford, Calif.: Stanford University Press.

Joachimides, Christos, and Norman Rosenthal. 1993. *American Art in the Twentieth Century: Painting and Sculpture 1913–1993.* New York: Prestel.

Johnson, James. 1995. *Listening in Paris.* Berkeley: University of California Press.

Jones, Timothy. 1999. *Beethoven: The "Moonlight" and Other Sonatas Op. 27 and Op. 31.* Cambridge: Cambridge University Press.

Jordanova, Ludmilla. 1989. *Sexual Visions: Images of Gender in Science and Medicine between the 18th and 20th Centuries.* London: Harvester.

Juslin, P., and J. Sloboda, eds. 2001. *Music and Emotion: Theory and Research.* Oxford: Oxford University Press.

Katz, Jack. 1996. "The Social Psychology of Adam and Eve." *Theory and Society* 25, no. 4: 545–82.

Khan, Azizur, and Carl Riskin. 2001. *Inequality and Poverty in China in the Age of Globalization.* New York: Oxford University Press.

Korpe, Marie. 2004. *Shoot the Singer: Music Censorship Today.* London: Zed Books.

Kraus, Richard 1989. *Pianos and Politics in China: Middle-Class Ambitions and the Struggle over Western Music.* New York: Oxford University Press.

———. 1991. *Brushes with Power: Modern Politics and the Chinese Art of Calligraphy.* Berkeley: University of California Press.

————. 1995. "Introduction: Urban Culture and Identities." In *Urban Spaces in Contemporary China: The Potential for Autonomy and Community in Post-Mao China,* ed. Deborah Davis et al. Washington, D.C.: Woodrow Wilson Center Press; New York: Cambridge University Press.

————. 2004. *The Party and the Arty in China: The New Politics of Culture.* Lanham, Md.: Rowman & Littlefield.

Kris, Ernst, and Otto Kurz. 1979. *Legend, Myth and Magic in the Image of the Artist: A Historical Experiment.* New Haven, Conn.: Yale University Press.

Kubler, George. 1962. *The Shape of Time: Remarks on the History of Things.* New Haven, Conn.: Yale University Press.

Kulka, Tomas. 1996. *Kitsch and Art.* University Park: Pennsylvania State University Press.

Laing, R. D. 1965. *The Divided Self.* Harmondsworth, U.K.: Penguin.

Landon, H. C. Robbins. 1970. *Beethoven: A Documentary Study.* New York: Macmillan.

————. 1976–80. *Haydn: Chronicle and Works* (5 vols.). Bloomington: Indiana University Press.

Lavater, Johann Caspar. 1844. *Essays on Physiognomy.* Trans. T. Holcroft. London: N.p.

Le Huray, Peter, and James Day. 1981. *Music and Aesthetics in the Eighteenth and Early-Nineteenth Centuries.* Cambridge: Cambridge University Press.

Leppert, R. 1993. *The Sight of Sound: Music, Representation, and the History of the Body.* Berkeley: University of California Press.

————. 1999. "Cultural Contradiction, Idolatry, and the Piano Virtuoso: Franz Liszt." In *Piano Roles: Three Hundred Years of Life with the Piano,* ed. J. Parakilas. New Haven, Conn.: Yale University Press.

Little, Meredith, and Natalie Jenne. 2001. *Dance and the Music of J. S. Bach.* Bloomington: Indiana University Press.

Macdonald, R., D. Hargreaves, and D. Miell, eds. 2002. *Musical Identities.* Oxford: Oxford University Press.

Madsen, Richard. 1998. *China's Catholics: Tragedy and Hope in an Emerging Civil Society.* Berkeley: University of California Press.

Maffesoli, Michel. 1996. *A Time of the Tribes.* London: Sage.

Mahlendorf, Ursula R. 1985. *The Wellsprings of Literary Creation.* Columbia, S.C.: Camden House.

Marion, Jean-Luc. 2002. *In Excess: Studies of Saturated Phenomena.* Trans. R. Horner and V. Berraud. New York: Fordham University Press.

Marquis, Alice Goldfarb. 2002. *Marcel Duchamp: The Bachelor Stripped Bare.* Boston: MFA Publications.

Martin, Peter J. 1995. *Sounds and Society: Themes in the Sociology of Music.* Manchester: Manchester University Press.

————. 2002. "Over the Rainbow? On the Quest for 'the Social' in Musical Analysis." *Journal of the Royal Musical Association* 127: 130–46.

McClary, Susan. 1991. *Feminine Endings.* Minneapolis: University of Minnesota Press.

————. 2000. *Conventional Wisdom: The Content of Musical Form.* Berkeley: University of California Press.

McCormick, L. 2000. "*Hommage à Sacher:* A Case Study in the Commissioning, Composition, and Performance of New Music in the 1970s." Unpublished M.Phil. thesis, Oxford University.

———. 2003. "Constructing Culture: Women Patrons and the Concert Halls of Los Angeles." *Yale Journal of Sociology* 3: 133–54.

McKeon, Richard. 1972. "History and Philosophy. Art and Science, Validity and Truth." In *Truth and Historicity,* ed. H. G. Gadamer. The Hague: Martinus Nijoff.

Menand, Louis. 1988. "Lives of the Saints." *The New Republic,* October 31, 34.

Moens-Haenen, G. n.d. "Vibrato." In *Grove Music Online,* ed. L. Macy. www.grovemusic.com.

Morley, David. 1997. "Theoretical Orthodoxies: Textualism, Constructivism and the 'New Ethnography' in Cultural Studies." In *Cultural Studies in Question,* ed. Marjorie Ferguson and Peter Golding. London: Sage.

Newman, Barnett. 1992. *Barnett Newman: Selected Writings and Interviews,* ed. John P. O'Neill. Berkeley: University of California Press.

Nuridsany, Michel. 2004. *L'Art contemporain chinois* [Contemporary Chinese Art]. Paris: Flammarion.

Nussbaum, Martha. 1995. *Poetic Justice.* Boston: Beacon.

Oliva, Achille Bonito. 2002. *Art Tribes.* Milan: Skira.

Ormond, Rosalie. 2003. *The Soul: A History.* Stoud: Sutton.

Pavlicevic, M., and G. Ansdell, eds. 2004. *Community Music Therapy.* London: Kingsley.

Peterson, Richard. 1994. "The Production Perspective." In *The Sociology of Culture,* ed. Diana Crane. Cambridge, Mass.: Blackwell.

———. 1997. *Creating Country Music: Fabricating Authenticity.* Chicago: University of Chicago Press.

Peterson, Richard, and N. Anand. 2004. "The Production of Culture Perspective." *Annual Review of Sociology* 30: 311–34.

Peterson, Richard, and D. Berger. 1975. "Cycles in Symbol Production: The Case of Popular Music." *American Sociological Review* 40: 158–73.

Poggioli, Renato. 1968. *The Theory of the Avant-Garde.* Trans. G. Fitzgerald. Cambridge, Mass.: Harvard University Press.

Pohl, Frances. 2002. *Framing America.* New York: Thames & Hudson.

Polcari, Stephen. 1993. "Modernist History and Surrealist Imagination: American Art in the 1940s." In *American Art in the Twentieth Century: Painting and Sculpture 1913–1993,* ed. C. Joachimides et al. Berlin: Zeitgeist-Gesellschaft.

Pollack, Barbara. 2004. "Mainland Dreams on Tape." *Art in America,* June/July, 130.

Pollock, Griselda. 1980. "Artists, Mythologies and Media Genius: Madness Art History." *Screen* 21: 57–96.

Rank, Otto. 1989. *Art and Artist: Creative Urge and Personality Development.* New York: Norton.

Ricoeur, Paul. 1984. *Time and Narrative.* Trans. Kathleen McLaughlin and David Pellauer. Chicago: University of Chicago Press.

Roy, William. 2003. "Who Shall Not Be Moved? Folk Music, Community and Race in the American Communist Party and the Highlander School." Paper presented to the Sociology of Culture Session on Politics, Strategy and Culture, American Sociological Association Meetings, Atlanta.

Ruud, Even. 2002. "Music as Cultural Immogen—Three Narratives on the Use of Music as a Technology of Health." In *Research in and for Higher Music Education,* ed. I. M. Hanken et al. Festschrift for Harald Jørgensen. Oslo: Norwegian Academy of Music.

Schein, Louisa. 2001. "Urbanity, Cosmopolitanism, Consumption." In *China Urban: Ethnographies of Contemporary China,* ed. Suzanne Z. Gottschang and Lyn Jeffrey. Durham, N.C.: Duke University Press.

Senner, Wayne M. 1999. *The Critical Reception of Beethoven's Compositions by His German Contemporaries, Vol. 1.* Lincoln: University of Nebraska Press.

Sherwood, Steven J. 1998. "Theorizing the Enigma: The Problem of the Soul in Durkheim's *Elementary Forms of the Religious Life.*" *Epoche: University of California Journal for the Study of Religions* 21, no. 2: 47–56.

———. 2002. "The Sacred and Profane Artist: Narrating John Lennon." PhD diss., University of California, Los Angeles.

Shils, Edward. 1975. *Center and Periphery: Essays in Macrosociology.* Chicago: University of Chicago Press.

Shiner, Larry. 2001. *The Invention of Art.* Chicago: University of Chicago Press.

Shookman, Ellis. 1993. *The Faces of Physiognomy: Interdisciplinary Approaches to Johann Caspar Lavater.* Columbia, S.C.: Camden House.

Simmel, Georg. 2005. *Rembrandt.* New York: Routledge. Originally published in 1916.

Simms, Bryan R., ed. 1999. *Composers on Modern Musical Culture: An Anthology of Readings on Twentieth-Century Music.* New York: Schirmer Books.

Singerman, Howard. 1999. *Art Subjects: Making Artists in the American University.* Berkeley: University of California Press.

Small, Christopher. 1998. *Musicking: The Meanings of Performing and Listening.* Hanover, N.H.: Wesleyan University Press.

Solie, Ruth, ed. 1993. *Musicology and Difference.* Berkeley: University of California Press.

Stevens, Mark, and Annalyn Swan. 2004. *De Kooning: An American Master.* New York: Knopf.

Stravinsky, Igor. 2003. *Poetics of Music: In the Form of Six Lessons.* Trans. A. Knodel and I. Dah. Cambridge, Mass.: Harvard University Press. Originally published in 1942.

Tang, Wenfang, and William Parish. 2000. *Chinese Urban Life under Reform.* Cambridge: Cambridge University Press.

Taruskin, R. 1995. *Text and Act: Essays on Music and Performance.* New York: Oxford University Press.

Taylor, Diana. 1997. *Disappearing Acts.* Durham, N.C.: Duke University Press.

Temperly, Nicholas, and Peter Wollny. n.d. "Bach Revival." In *Grove Music Online,* ed. L. Macy. www.grovemusic.com.

Thayer, Alexander Wheelock. 1967. *Thayer's Life of Beethoven,* 2 vols., rev. and ed. by Elliott Forbes. Princeton, N.J.: Princeton University Press.

Vine, Richard. 2004. "Sixty Ways of Looking at China." *Art in America,* June/July, 124.

Wallace, Robin. 1986. *Beethoven's Critics.* Cambridge: Cambridge University Press.

Watt, Ian. 1957. *The Rise of the Novel.* Berkeley: University of California Press.

Webster, James. 1997. "The Creation, Haydn's Late Vocal Music, and the Musical Sublime." In *Haydn and His World,* ed. E. Sisman. Princeton, N.J.: Princeton University Press.

Wegeler, F., and F. Ries. 1987. "Biographical Notes." *Beethoven Reconsidered,* trans. F. Noonan. Arlington, Va.: Great Ocean Publishers.

Whelan, Richard. 1995. *Alfred Stieglitz A Biography.* Boston: Little, Brown.

Whitman, Walt. 1959. *Leaves of Grass.* New York: Penguin. Originally published in 1855.

Witkin, Robert. 1995. *Art and Social Structure.* Cambridge: Polity.

———. 1997. "Constructing a Sociology for an Icon of Aesthetic Modernity: *Olympia* Revisited." *Sociological Theory* 15, no. 2: 101–25.

———. 1998. *Adorno on Music.* London: Routledge.

———. 2005. "A New Paradigm for a Sociology of Aesthetics." In *The Sociology of Art: Ways of Seeing,* ed. David Inglis and John Hughson. New York: Palgrave Macmillan.

Witmer, Robert, and Anthony Marks. "Cover." In *Grove Music Online,* ed. L. Macy. www.grovemusic.com.

Wu, Hung. 2000. *Exhibiting Experimental Art in China.* Chicago: Smart Museum of Art, University of Chicago.

Wu, Hung, and Christopher Phillips. 2004. *Between Past and Future: New Photography and Video from China.* Chicago: Smart Museum of Art, University of Chicago; New York: International Center of Photography; Göttingen, Germany: Steidl.

Yan, Yunxiang. 2000. "Of Hamburger and Social Space: Consuming McDonald's in Beijing." In *The Consumer Revolution in Urban China,* ed. Deborah Davis. Berkeley: University of California Press.

Zhu, Qi. 2001. "Do Westerners Really Understand Chinese Avant-Garde Art?" In *Chinese Art at the End of the Millennium,* ed. John Clark. Beijing: New Art Media Press.

Index

Page locators in italics refer to figures.

abstract expressionism, 6, 36, 38, 41–42, 49–50, 93

abstraction, 42–43; late capitalism societies and, 46–47; self-critique and, 41–42

actors, 125–26

Adorno, Theodor, 2, 24–25, 33, 36, 48, 74–75, 128; *Dialectic of Enlightenment,* 21–22, 23, 40; "On the Social Situation of Music," 40

advertising, 3

aesthetic response, 24–25, 32

aesthetics, 11; collective mode of experience, 18, 32–33, 33–34n2; historical development of, 16–17; as socially situated, 75

aesthetics, as term, 24

African Americans, 30

After Song Dynasty Zhao Ji "Loquat and Bird" (Hong), 63–64, *65*

agency, 10; discourse of, 105–6; inner life, concept of, 106–11, 117; music as medium for, 103–4, 118

Alarm Will Sound, 131

Alexander, Jeffrey C., 33, 82–83, 96, 99, 122, 133, 138

Allgemeine Musicalische Zeitung, 108–9

Alloway, Lawrence, 37

American art, national project of, 30–31

American Renaissance, 93

architecture, 130–31

art: as achievement concept, 17–18; definitions of, 16–17; as derived from religion, 85–86; as form of cognition, 19–22; as revelatory medium, 92; as social activity, 19, 32; submersion in life, 36–37, 48–49

Art (journal), 55

art agents, 68–72

Art and Culture (Greenberg), 37–38, *49*

Art and Social Structure (Witkin), 5–6, 37

Art and Soul (Flack), 92

art appreciation, 16

art coefficient, 89

art hero, 10, 82, 94–95, 97; Beethoven hero, 105, 106–12

art history, 1–2, 4–5

artist: autonomy of, 8, 16–17, 32, 36–37, 40, 47, 70, 75; creative process and, 87–91, 99–100; cult of, 84, 86; cultural sociology of, 100–101; cultural structure of, 94–95, 97, 101; dreamtime and, 92–93; higher purpose required of, 96, 98; as individual, 41–42; isolation of, 8, 36–37, 40–41, 110; marginality of, 36, 40; myth of, 9, 94–95; resistance, struggle

artist *(continued)*
  with, 90; as ritual figure, 99–101;
  as sacred/spiritual figure, 82–84,
  91–93; as seeker of the sacred,
  84–87; self-understanding, 22,
  41–42, 95–96; theory of, 81–82;
  transformation of, 97–98
artist biography, 93–98, 124;
  romance of expression, 96–97;
  transformation of artist, 97–98
artist industry, 14, 83. *See also*
  culture industry
art object, 23–24
artwork, sociology of, 5, 142
art world, 16, 19, 83
art worlds approach, 2, 5, 11,
  140–41
audience, 13; changes in culture
  of listening, 110–11, 128–29;
  domestic, for Chinese avant-garde
  art, 55–56, 69, 71; fragmentation
  of, 126–27; performance and,
  126–29; production of meaning
  and, 15–16, 21–23, 32; response,
  24–25, 32; ritual practices of, 86,
  90; social power and, 139; truth-
  bearing capacity of art, 6–7, 21–22
aura, 34n2
Australian aboriginal tribes, 84, 87,
  89, 91, 92, 101
authenticity, 4, 52, 72, 126, 134–36
authentistic approach, 136, 144n6
autonomous art, 76, 79n10
autonomy of artist, 8, 32, 36–37,
  40, 47, 70; institutionalization of,
  16–17, 75
"Avant-Garde and Kitsch"
  (Greenberg), 39–40
avant-garde art, 8, 17 (*see also* Chinese
  avant-garde art); 1950s, 25–26;
  1960s, 42, 49–50; gesture art, 37–38;
  movements, 35–36; radical breaks,
  38–39; as term, 76–77n1; toward
  meaningful sociology of, 74–76

Babbitt, Milton, 127–28
Bach, J. S., 128, 135

Bachelard, Gaston, 99, 101
background symbols, 124–25;
  audience and, 126–27
Bang on a Can, 131
Barthes, Roland, 14
Beatles, 90, 91, 97
Becker, Howard, 4, 140–41
Beethoven, Ludwig van, 10, 17,
  103; C-minor Piano Concerto
  no. 3, 109; compositional
  style, 105; Fifth Symphony,
  109–10; gendered performances
  of, 113–16, 118n4; musical
  critical discourse on, 108–10;
  performance practice, 116–17;
  as point of reference for agency,
  105–6; self-composition, 110–12;
  Violin Sonatas op. 23 and 24, 108
Beethoven hero, concept of, 105,
  106–12
Beethoven Hero (Burnham), 105
Benjamin, Walter, 34n2, 74–75
Berlinische Musikalische Zeitung,
  107–8
Bernard, Frau, 113
Bernel, Robert, 69
biography. *See* artist biography
bodily performance, 112–13, 117–18;
  Beethoven's performance practice,
  116–17; gender and, 10, 113–16,
  118. *See also* performance practice
book as object, 37
Book from the Sky, A (Xu), 57–59
Bourdieu, Pierre, 1, 5, 7, 27, 75–76,
  79n19, 138
bourgeois society, 44–45, 47–48
branding, 14
Britten, Benjamin, 126, 128
Bryson, Norman, 5
Burger, Peter, 17, 40, 48–49, 74
Burnham, Scott, 105, 110–11

Cai Guoqiang, 68
Calgary International Organ
  Competition, 124
canonical works, 5
capitalist society, late, 46–47

CBGB, 131, 143n2
Cello Concerto (Elgar), 137
censorship, 28
Cézanne, Paul, 41
Chen Yifei, 55–56
China: Cultural Revolution, 54, 55, 73, 78nn5, 8; political history, 8–9, 51–55, 67, 77n2
China/Avant-Garde Exhibition, 55
Chinese art institutions, 56
Chinese avant-garde art, 8–9, 51–52; art agents and, 68–72; authenticity, discourse of, 52, 72; demystification of West, 8–9, 60–66, 73–74; domestic audience for, 55–56, 69, 71; exhibitions, 55, 67 68, 78–79n10; gaudy/pretty art, 64–65; grand narratives in, 59, 66; market and, 52, 62–64, 69–74; meaning of style and cultural-pragmatic dissonance, 72–74; post-1989 postmodern shift, 60–66, 72–74; pre-1989, 55–59; realism vs. abstraction, 56–58; social meaning of modern style, 52–54; transformations around 1989, 67–68; West as pragmatic resource, 68–72; Western modernist style appropriated, 55–56, 59
Chinese Communist Party (CCP), 67
Chinese modernism, 77–78n2, 78n3; first-wave, 52–53; second-wave, 54; third-wave, 52, 55–59
Chinese National Art Gallery, 55
Clark, T. J., 5
classical social theory, 5–6, 14, 82
coactional domain, 46
cognitive praxis, art as, 19–22
Cold War, 73
collective consciousness, 83, 94
collective mode of aesthetic experience, 18, 32–33, 33–34n2
collective representations, 97–99, 128; layered system, 123–25; social power and, 138

collectivities, 20, 33–34n2, 82
composer/performer phenomenon, 125–26
Concerning the Spiritual in Art (Kandinsky), 88
concert halls, 129–31, 143n1
concrete, 6, 23
conditioning, 15
confessional mode, 90
"Constructing Sociology for an Icon of Aesthetic Modernity: *Olympia* Revisited" (Witkin), 5–6
constructivist perspective, 4, 19–20
contact values, 43–44
convention, 140–41
Cook, Nicholas, 104, 121, 122
corroboree, 87, 91
Could, Glenn, 132
country music, 4
cover bands, 143n4
craft, vs. art, 15, 16
Crane, Diana, 4, 26, 75, 76, 79n20
creative process, 85–86, 87–91, 99–100
critical moment, 2–3
critics, 10
Critique of Judgement (Kant), 106–7
cubism, 45–46
cult of the artist, 84, 86
cult of the image, 86
cult of the individual, 92, 100
Cultural Revolution, 54, 55, 73, 78nn5, 8
cultural sociology, 82, 100–101
cultural structure of artist, 94–95, 97, 101
Cultural Studies (CS), 3, 33n2
culture, 7, 32; national, 29–30, 31; popular, 2–4, 34n2. *See also* production of culture perspective
culture industry, 2, 14–15, 21, 23, 33n1
culture of listening, 110–11, 128–29

Dadaists, 49
Dante, 89
Danto, Arthur, 30
decoding, 15

de Kooning, Willem, 24, 25–27,
    88–89
Dematte, Monica, 68
denigration of artist, 95
DeNora, Tia, 4, 10, 17, 23, 139
Dialectic of Enlightenment
    (Horkheimer and Adorno),
    21–22, 23, 40
dimensions, 13–14
disciplinary boundaries, 13–14
distal values, 43, 45
Distinction (Bourdieu), 138
Divine Comedy, The (Dante), 89
dreamtime, 92–93
Duchamp, Marcel, 37, 88
du Pré, Jacqueline, 137
Durkheim, Émile, 1, 9, 81–84,
    99–101; shift in late theory of, 82;
    soul, view of, 86–87; on spiritual
    force, 84–85
Dylan, Bob, 90, 91

Egyptian artists, 44
*Elementary Forms of Religious Life,
    The* (Durkheim), 9, 81–82,
    84–86, 99–101; "The Notion of
    the Soul," 86, 91
Elgar, Edward, 137
Elias, Norbert, 4, 17
embodiment, irony of, 96
Emerson, Ralph Waldo, 93
emotions: institutions composed of, 82
encoding, 14, 15, 22
England, emergence of pop art in, 37
Eroica quartet, 135
ethnomethodological approach, 142
"Exactly What Is It That Makes the
    Modern Home So Appealing"
    (Yu), 64–65
Excavation (de Kooning), 25, 26
exhibitions, 30; Chinese avant-garde
    art, 55, 67–68, 78–79n10
experience: collective mode of, 18,
    32–33, 33–34n2; perceptual
    modes and, 45–46, 49–50
expression, romance of, 96–98
expressive revolution, 90–91

Eyck, Jan van, 44
Eyerman, Ron, 7, 10, 101

false consciousness, 22, 31
Farber, Howard, 68–69
feminist theory, 3
Field of Cultural Production, The
    (Bourdieu), 75
Figes, Orlando, 19–20
film, 28
Flack, Audrey, 88, 92–93
Flaubert, Gustave, 27
flower bird painting, 63–64
force: creative process and, 88–90,
    100; imaginative, 85–86, 88–90;
    spiritual, 84–85, 88
*Forged Invitation Letter from an
    International Biennale* (Yan), 64,
    66
form, 22
formalism, 75, 79n19
Foucault, Michel, 1, 3, 4
framing, 15
Franco, Francisco, 28
Frankfurt School, 2, 3, 74–75
Freid, Michael, 39
French Revolution, 87, 97
Frye, Northrop, 96

Gadamer, Hans Georg, 23
Gao Minglu, 53, 54
gatekeepers, 26, 139
Geertz, Clifford, 81
Gehry, Frank, 131
gender, performance and, 10,
    113–16, 118
Gengjian Li, 56
genius, 4, 10
gesture art, 37–38
Goffman, Erving, 14–15
Goldman, Albert, 97–98
Gramsci, Antonio, 29
grand narrative, in Chinese avant-
    garde art, 59, 66
grand theory, 1, 6, 27
Greek myths, 95
Greenberg, Clement, 26, 37–42,

75; *Art and Culture,* 37–38, 49;
"Avant-Garde and Kitsch," 39–40
Greenberg (Latham), 8
Guangzhou Biennial, 67

Hall, Stuart, 22, 24
Hamilton, Richard, 37, 64
*Handbook for Piano Care and Good
Musicianship* (Streicher), 114–16
Handel, Georg Friedrich, 135–36
haptic mode of perception, 43–44
Hauser, Arnold, 44
Hegel, G. W. F., 47, 135
Heimovitz, Matt, 131
Helbling, Lorenz, 69
Henryz, F. D. P., 69
hero. *See* art hero
heroic, in music, 105, 106–12
high art, 2, 3, 20, 32
historical context, 6, 7, 15; Chinese
political history, 8–9, 51–55, 67,
77n2; definitions of art and, 16–17
Hoffman, E. T. A., 109–11
Hogwood, Christopher, 136
Hong Hao, 61–62
Hong Lei, 63–64, 65, 71
Hood, Margaret, 116
Hughes, Robert, 93
Hu Jiemin, 60
humanities, 1, 3, 123

ideals, 85–86, 92
ideology, 14
image, cult of, 86
images, political significance of,
29–31, 60, 65
imagination, 9; cultural, 99; sociological,
100–101; theory of, 85–86
imaginative space, 18–19, 32
Imagine: John Lennon, 97–98
immanent model, 9, 87–91
Independents, 37
individual, 18, 82; artist as, 41–42;
Beethoven as point of reference
for, 105–6; cult of, 92, 100
inner life, concept of, 106–11
innovation, 6

inspiration, 88–90, 92, 99
instrumentalism, 5, 20
instrument making, 132–33
interactional domain, 46, 47
international exhibitions, 30
Internet, Chinese artists and, 69,
70–71
interpretation, 4–5, 27–28
intra-actional domain, 46, 47, 49

Jamison, Andrew, 20, 101
Jefferson, Thomas, 29
Jian Zemin, 64
Judd, Donald, 39
"Just What Is It That Makes
Today's Homes So Attractive, So
Appealing?" (Hamilton), 37, 64

Kandinsky, Wassily, 88
Kant, Immanuel, 106–7, 110
Kennedy, Nigel, 132
kitsch, 39–40
knowledge claims, 20
Kris, Ernst, 94–95
Kurz, Otto, 94–95

labor, division of, 13, 141–42
Lacan, Jacques, 3
Laing, R. D., 48
Latham, John, 8, 37–39, 49, 50
Leaves of Grass (Whitman), 88
L'education sentimentale (Flaubert), 27
*Legend, Myth and Magic in the Image
of the Artist* (Kris and Kurz),
94–95
Lennon, John, 9, 90, 97–98
Leppert, Richard, 104–5, 117, 132
Lin Fengmian, 52, 53
linguistic turn, 3
Liszt, Franz, 104–5
Lin Haisu, 52, 53
Liu Jianhua, 60, *61*
Lives of Lennon, The (Goldman),
97–98
Lives of the Artists (Vasari), 94
"Lives of the Saints, The" (Menand),
98

London, Barbara, 69

Madrid film school, 28
Mae, Vanessa, 132
Maffesoli, Michel, 33–34n2
mana (spiritual force), 84–85, 88
Manet, Edouard, 5–6, 8, 40, 41
Mao Zedong, 64
Mao Zedong No. 1 (Wang), 56, *57*
Marcuse, Herbert, 2
Marion, Jean-Luc, 90
market, 24, 26, 30, 40; Chinese
    avant-garde art and, 52, 62–64,
    69–74
mass culture, 3, 21, 34n2, 39–40
McCormick, Lisa, 10–11, 103, 106,
    112
meaning, 7, 20–28; aesthetic
    action and, 11; approaches
    to, 14–15; bracketing of, 1, 2,
    142; as contextual, 19; fusion
    of performer with, 125; as
    interactive, 22–23, 32; multiple
    levels of, 3; performance and, 22–
    23, 122; performance perspective
    and, 11, 15; performance practice
    and, 134–37; preferred, 22;
    production of, 2, 14–16, 21–23,
    32; social construction of, 4,
    19–20; structure and, 82–83; in
    totalitarian regimes, 28; truth-
    bearing capacity of art, 6–7,
    21–22
Menand, Louis, 98
Mendelssohn, Felix, 135
Mesmer, Franz, 117
Messiah (Handel), 135–36
Metropolitan Museum of Art (New
    York), 30
Michaelis, C. F., 107–8, 118n2
Mills, C. Wright, 100
minimalism, 39
minorities, 30
mise-en-scène, 133–38, 142–43,
    144n7
modernism, 6–8; first strategy of,
    47–48; painting, 41; second
    strategy of, 48–50; self-critique,
    41–42; two faces of, 8, 36–37,
    47–49. *See also* Chinese avant-
    garde art; Chinese modernism
modern society, transition to, 5–6
moral power of soul, 91–92
movements, 7–8; avant-gardes as,
    35–36; of sixties, 42, 49–50
Mozart, Wolfgang Amadeus, 4, 17,
    113, 119n5
"Mr. Gnoh" (Hong), 61, *62*
"Mr. Hong" (Hong), 61–62
"Mr Hong Please come in" (Hong), *63*
Municipal Gallery of Modern Art
    (Dublin), 30
museums, 92
music, 4; critical moment in, 2–3; as
    medium for agency, 103–4, 118;
    new music, 127–28, 131, 132;
    role in social ordering, 103–3; as
    social performance, 10–11, 106,
    112, 121–23; total serialism,
    127–28
music, sociology of, 103–4, 121–22
musical critical discourse, 10, 106,
    107; on Beethoven, 108–10
Music and Social Movements
    (Eyerman and Jamison), 20
music competitions, 124
musician, as art hero, 105, 106–12
musicology, 121–24
"My America" (Zhang), 71, 72
"My Australia" (Zhang), 71
"My New York" (Zhang), 71
myth, 7, 9, 29, 94–95; of music
    performance, 124–25; schools of
    art, 92–93

Nanjing Massacre, 65
narrative, 96; grand, 1, 59, 66; rise
    and fall scenario, 94, 95–97
National Academy of Design (New
    York), 30
national galleries, 30
Newman, Barnett, 42
new music, 127–28, 131, 132
new musicology, 124

Nochlin, Linda, 5
novel, 15–16, 27–28

Olympia (Manet), 5–6, 8
Ono, Yoko, 97
"On the Social Situation of Music"
   (Adorno), 40
Opium War, 53
optic mode of perception, 44–45
optimistic tradition, 95

Paganini, Nicolo, 144n7
Painted over Rocks (Wu), 56, *58*
painting, modernist, 41
Paradis, Maria Theresa, 117
Parsons, Talcott, 90
perceptual modes: haptic, 43–44;
   optic, 44–45; somatic, 8, 44–47
perceptual-realist art, 43, 45
performance, 7, 103–4; actors,
   125–26; appearance of performer,
   117–18, 131–32; audience and,
   126–29; background symbols,
   124–25; bodily procedures, 112–
   17; collective identity and, 20;
   as dramaturgical, 112; elements
   of, 122, 123–40; gender and, 10,
   113–16, 118; instrument making,
   132–33; meaning and, 11, 15,
   22–23, 122, 134–37; means of
   symbolic production, 129–33;
   mise-en-scène, 133–38, 142–43,
   144n7; musical scripts, 123,
   143–44n5; myths of, 124–25;
   public/private dichotomy and,
   124; recording technology, 126,
   128–29, 132; social power, 11,
   138–40, 143; style and, 133–35,
   143–44n5
performance perspective, 10–11,
   141–43; collective representations,
   layered system of, 123–25; meaning
   and, 11, 15; outline of, 123–40
performance practice, 134–37, 141.
   See also bodily performance
performance traditions, 137, 141
persistence, 89

pessimistic tradition, 95
Peterson, Richard, 4, 140
phenomenological approach, 9
Philharmonic Hall (Berlin), 131
physiognomy, 10, 117
piano, 10, 112–13
Picasso, Pablo, 45
Play (Liu), 60, *61*
Poggioli, Renato, 35–36, 74
Pohl, Frances, 29
Polcari, Stephen, 18–19
politics and art, 28–31; Chinese
   political history, 8–9, 51–55, 67,
   77n2; national culture and, 29–30,
   31; new nations and, 30–31
pop art, 36, 42, 49–50, 93; Chinese,
   64–65; religious dynamic in,
   90–91; as term, 37; transition to,
   7–8, 36–37
popular culture, 2–4, 34n2
postmodernism, 6, 39
poststructural discourse analysis, 3–4
potential of art, 24–25
power, 4, 83; social, 11, 138–40, 143
presence, 23
primitive consciousness, 48
production, 4; of meaning, 2, 14–16,
   21–23, 32; means of symbolic,
   129–33
realism of, 96; of value, 1–2
production/consumption paradigm,
   1, 10–11, 14, 21, 121, 140–41
production of culture perspective,
   1–2, 6, 17, 20–21, 26, 75–76,
   140–41
proximal values, 43, 45–46
public/private structure, 124

quotation images, 49

radio, 128
Raft of Medusa (Hu), 60
Rank, Otto, 93–94
realism, 42, 96, 100; in Chinese
   style, 56–58; socialist style of, 54,
   73, 78n5

recording technology, 126, 128–29, 132
reflection, 24
Reich, Steve, 131
religion: imagination and, 85–86; model of social order and, 82–83; popular art and, 90–91; sacred/profane dichotomy, 84, 86, 90–91, 96. *See also* sacred/profane dichotomy; soul
Rembrandt (Simmel), 5
Renaissance artists, 43, 44–45
representation, 20; collective, 97–99, 123–25, 128, 138
reputation, 4, 138–39
resistance, 3, 90, 99
Revere, Paul, 29
Richardson, John, 98
Ricoeur, Paul, 96, 101
rise and fall scenario, 94, 95–97
ritual conduct, 82–84, 86, 90, 122
romance of expression, 96–98
romantic/idealist tradition, 20–21, 75, 109–10
Ronald McDonald image, 60, 65
Rostropovich, Mstislav, 135, 139
Rules of Art (Bourdieu), 75

sacred, as term, 84
sacred/profane dichotomy, 84, 86, 90–91, 96
St. Martins College of Art and Design, 37–38
St. Matthew Passion (Bach), 135
salvation, 92
Savitt, Scott, 69
Scharoun, Hans, 131
Schiller, Friedrich, 107, 110
Schoenberg, Arnold, 21, 23
schools of art, 92–93
Schumann, Robert, 105
scripts, musical, 123, 143–44n5
self-awareness, 106
semiotic analysis, 6
Senner, William, 108, 109
sent-down movement, 54
sentimental art, 107–8, 110

Seven Chinese Intellectuals in a Bamboo Forest, 60, 78n9
Seven Chinese Intellectuals in a Bamboo Forest (Yang), 60–61
Seyfried, Ignaz, 117
Sgt. Pepper's Lonely Hearts Club Band (Beatles), 90, 91
Shanghai Biennial, 67, 68
Sherwood, Steven J., 9
Shils, Edward, 85
Shiner, Larry, 16
Shostakovich, Dmitri, 19–20
Sigg, Uli, 68
signifying practices, 14
Silver Factory, 91, 93, 98
Simmel, Georg, 5
Singerman, Howard, 18
Smith, Karen, 69, 70
socialist realist style, 54, 73, 78n5
sociality, 33–34n2
social performance: defined, 122; music as, 10–11, 106, 112, 121–23. *See also* performance; performance perspective
social power, 11, 138–40, 143
society: bourgeois, 44–45, 47–48; creative power of, 85–86; spiritual model of, 9, 85–86, 87; transition to modern, 5–6
sociology of music, 103–4, 121–22
sociology of the arts, 1–2, 14; steps toward meaningful, 31–33, 74–76
somatic level of perception, 8, 44–47
soul, 9, 86–87; immanent model of, 87–91; as manifestation of totemic principle, 87–88; moral power of, 91–92; transcendent model of, 87, 91–98. *See also* religion
South Africa, 30
Soviet Union, 54, 73
spatial metaphor, 7, 9, 10, 18–19
spiritual force *(mana),* 84–85, 88
spiritual model of society, 9, 85–86, 87
Star Group, 55
Stevens, Mark, 25

Stevens, Wallace, 100
Stieglitz, Alfred, 31
"Story of the Sony Walkman, The"
    (du Gay et al.), 14
Stravinsky, Igor, 23, 126, 128,
    143n3
Streicher, Andreas, 113, 114, 115–16
structuralism, subjective, 82, 96
structure: cultural, of artist, 94–95,
    97, 101; meaning and, 82–83
style, 6, 133–35, 143–44n5; Chinese
    avant-garde art and, 52–59,
    72–74; performance and, 133–35,
    143–44n5; socialist realist, 54, 73,
    78n5; social meaning of modern,
    52–54; Western modernist,
    55–56, 59
subject, 6, 36, 46–48
subjective structuralism, 82, 96
sublime, 106–11
Swan, Annalyn, 25
symbolic capital, 138–39
symbolic interactionist tradition,
    14–15
symbolic-pragmatic dissonance, 72
symbolic production, 129–33
symbols, 6; background, 124–27

Tang Song, 55
Taruskin, R., 136–37
teaching of art, 17–18
Thayer, A. W., 116
Theory of the Avant-Garde, The
    (Poggioli), 35–36
thick description, 4, 26
three-dimensional space, 46
Three-Year Starvation, 54
Tiananmen student movement, 51,
    67
time, 96
Tomashek, Johann Wenzel, 109
totalitarian regimes, 28
totality, art as, 24
total serialism, 127–28
totem, 84, 86
totemic principle, 83, 84–85, 91;
    soul as manifestation of, 87–88

tradition, 23–24
transcendent model, 9, 18–19, 87,
    91–98
transformation, 97–98
Trumbull, John, 29–30, 31
truth, 26–28
truth-bearing capacity of art, 6–7,
    21–22

Uncle McDonald Enters the Village,
    65–66

value, production of, 1–2
Van Gogh, Vincent, 88, 89
Vasari, Giorgi, 94
vibrato, 134–35, 141
Viennese context, 10
Virgin in the Church (van Eyck), 44
visual culture, 4–5
vitalistic approach, 136

Wagner, Richard, 105
Wallace, Brian, 69
Wallace, Robin, 108
Walt Disney Concert Hall, 131
Wang Guangyi, 56, *57*
Wang Qingsong, 60
Warhol, Andy, 9, 37, 91, 93, 98
Watt, Ian, 15–16
West: condemned by Chinese state,
    54; demystification of, 8–9,
    60–66, 73–74; as resource, 59,
    68–72
Whitman, Walt, 88
"Who Cares If You Listen? (The
    Composer as Specialist)"
    (Babbitt), 127–28
whole/fragment dichotomy, 24
Witkin, Robert, 5–8, 37
Wolper, David, 97–98
Woodstock, 91
Wu Sanzhuan, 56, *58*

Xiao Lu, 55
X Series: No. 4 (Zhang), 56, *58*
Xu Beihong, 52, 53
Xu Bing, 57–59, 68

Yang Fudong, 60–61
Yan Lei, 64, *66*
Yu Hanyou, 64–65

Zhang, Julia Chi, 8–9
Zhang Huan, 71–72
Zhang Peili, 56, *58*
Zhu Qi, 62, 70

About the Contributors

Tia DeNora is professor of sociology of music at Exeter University. She is the author of *Beethoven and the Construction of Genius* (California 1995/Fayard 1998), *Music in Everyday Life* (Cambridge 2000), and *After Adorno: Rethinking Music Sociology* (Cambridge 2003). Her current research focuses on material culture in Beethoven's Vienna and, in collaboration with music therapists, on music and health.

Ron Eyerman is professor of sociology and Director of the Center for Cultural Sociology (with Jeffrey Alexander) at Yale University. He has written extensively on collective identity and social movements, a large part of which concerns the arts and popular culture. His current research is about the murder of the Dutch filmmaker Theo van Gogh.

Lisa McCormick is a Ph.D. candidate in the Department of Sociology at Yale University. After completing a B.Mus. in cello performance and a B.A. in sociology at Rice University, she attended Oxford University as a Rhodes Scholar (Prairies & Corpus Christi 1998) where she received a Master of Philosophy in music. An accomplished cellist and proponent of new music, she has participated in new music programs at the Aspen Music Festival and the Britten-Pears School for Advanced Musical Studies, and she has performed in the Warsaw Autumn Festival.

Steve Sherwood is a cultural sociologist who currently lectures at UCLA where he received his doctorate in 2002. His current areas of interest include Andy Warhol and Pop as a cultural movement as well as the sociology of imagination.

Robert W. Witkin is professor of sociology at the University of Exeter. He has written extensively on the sociology of the arts. He is the author of *The Intelligence of Feeling* (Heinemann Educational Books 1974), *Art and Social Structure* (Polity 1995), *Adorno on Music* (Routledge

1998), and *Adorno on Popular Culture* (Routledge, Taylor-Francis 2003). His book *Artful Agency: Studies in Aesthetic Modernity* is to be published by TCS Sage in 2006.

Julia Chi Zhang is a doctoral candidate in the Department of Sociology at Yale University. Her interests include sociology of arts, cultural sociology, and social theory. Her previous research projects examine the myriad practices and consequences of cultural imperialism under globalization, in forms of "global consumerism," "global aesthetics," and "global justice."